MICHAEL SMITH HAS MASTERED THE MANY MIRACULOUS WAYS THAT WOOD, FIRE, AND SMOKE GO BEYOND MERELY COOKING FOOD, ELEVATING IT INSTEAD TO CRAVE-WORTHY MEALS. GATHERING WOOD, BUILDING A FIRE, TENDING IT, AND COOKING DELICIOUS FOOD WITH IT ALSO OFFERS US A CONNECTION TO THE PRIMAL ART OF COOKING OVER FIRE.

Wood, Fire & Smoke is a celebration of the intoxicating power of live-fire cooking. In over 80 recipes, the book explores the many ways to cook with fire—methods include wood-grilled, wood-smoked, wood oven–roasted (or baked), pit-smoked, plancha-seared, fire-kissed, barbecued, and charcoal-cooked. Cooking fires, each with its own purpose, are featured throughout and include wood ovens, offset smokers, rotisserie rigs, grills, campfires, wood candles, and more.

Inside, Smith shares his knowledge and cooking techniques for building and tending every type of cooking fire as well as how to harness the magical power of smoke—hard-earned experience cooking over a myriad of fires at the award-winning wood-fired culinary experience at the picturesque Inn at Bay Fortune. The cookbook features flavour-packed recipes for every backyard cook, including Smoked Cracked Ribs with Old-School Dry Rub; Wood-Roasted Pork Loin with Roasted Sweet Potatoes and Apples, and Wilted Arugula; Smoke-Roasted Chicken Wings with Ancho Spice Rub and Blue Cheese Aioli; Ember-Roasted Caveman Ribeye Steaks with Board Sauce; Hay-Smoked Salmon with Maritime Mustard Pickles; Iron-Steamed Mussels with Tomato Basil Broth and Fire Toast, Wood Oven–Fired Pizza; Fire-Kissed Broccoli Salad with Broccoli Hummus; Garlic Thyme Campfire Potatoes; Ember-Roasted Acorn Squash with Tarragon Applesauce; and Rum Creamsicle Campfire Marshmallows.

Wood, Fire & Smoke is for everyone who wants to cook over fire—novice and experienced cooks alike.

WOOD,
FIRE &
SMOKE

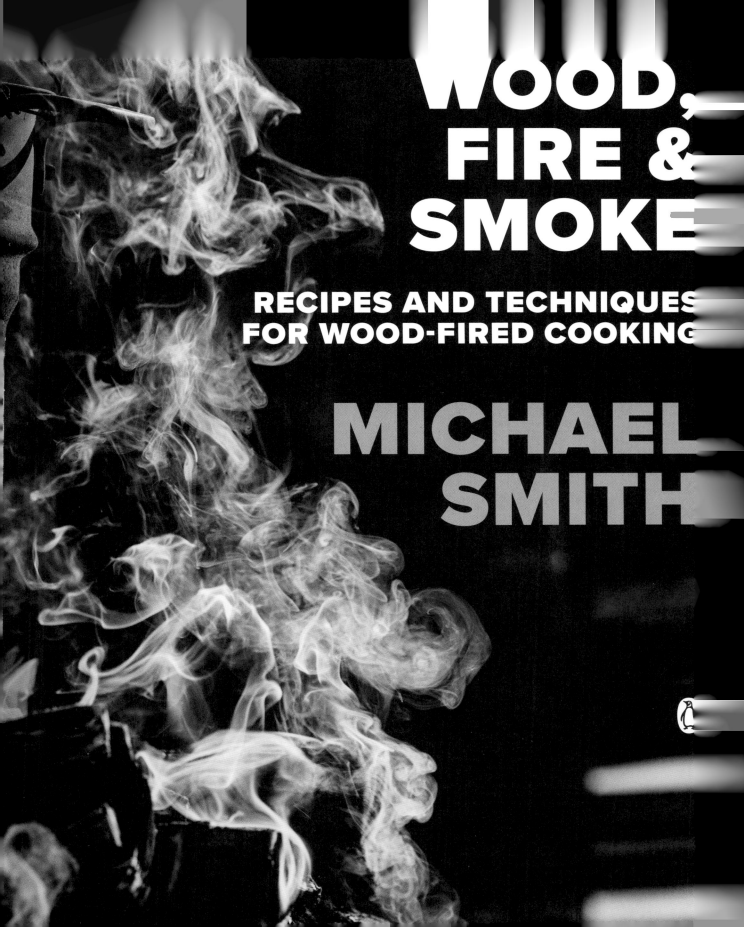

WOOD, FIRE & SMOKE

RECIPES AND TECHNIQUES
FOR WOOD-FIRED COOKING

MICHAEL SMITH

PENGUIN
an imprint of Penguin Canada, a division of Penguin Random House Canada Limited

Canada • USA • UK • Ireland • Australia • New Zealand • India • South Africa • China

First published 2025

www.penguinrandomhouse.ca

Library and Archives Canada Cataloguing in Publication

Title: Wood, fire & smoke : recipes and techniques for wood-fired cooking / Michael Smith.
Other titles: Wood, fire and smoke
Names: Smith, Michael, 1966 October 13- author.
Description: Includes index.
Identifiers: Canadiana (print) 20240372018 | Canadiana (ebook) 20240372026 | ISBN 9780735247222 (hardcover) | ISBN 9780735247239 (EPUB)
Subjects: LCSH: Outdoor cooking. | LCSH: Barbecuing. | LCSH: Fireplace cooking. | LCGFT: Cookbooks.
Classification: LCC TX823 .S65 2025 | DDC 641.5/78—dc23

Cover and interior design by Matthew Flute
Typeset by Terra Page
Recipe development by Chris Gibb
Food styling by Adrianna Remlinger
Photography by Al Douglas

Printed in China

10 9 8 7 6 5 4 3 2 1

Penguin
Random House
PENGUIN CANADA

TO ALL DRAWN
TO THE BRIGHT
WARMTH, PRIMAL
FLAVOURS,
AND ENDLESS
STORIES OF A
COOKING FIRE.

CONTENTS

THE RECIPES

INTRODUCTION

The day after humankind mastered fire, somebody took the heat and started cooking. We've never looked back. Today, gathering wood, building a fire, tending it, and cooking with it offers a primal connection to how life was once lived. A fire takes us forward by keeping us in the moment.

I enjoy my modern appliances as much at home and work as any digitally savvy cook and revel in the technical details and tasty results of precision cooking. But technology can be a double-edged sword. Gear designed simply for convenience and speed distances the cook from the process, removing the need for the essential human touch. For many cooks the antidote is fire.

Cooking with live fire demands and rewards our presence. You can't call it in; you must show up, and when you do you discover the joy of the moment, the beauty of focusing on something other than yourself, the strength that draws you along as you learn, even master, its power. The feeling is intoxicating, the results utterly delicious, and the flames always a spark for a gathering.

Throughout my lifetime of cooking and travel, I've tasted many miraculous ways that wood, fire, and smoke go beyond merely cooking food, elevating it instead to the heights of crave-worthy cuisine. I've met many cooks along the way who share an intense passion for our craft and love the Zen of the hot zone. At home I've gathered many a crowd around the spectacle and flavours of our hearth and backyard wood fire. All these things led to our legendary wood-fired culinary experience at the Inn at Bay Fortune and, ten years later, this book.

We build at least a dozen cooking fires daily at the inn, each with its own purpose and personality. We've learned so much through our own hard-earned and imaginative experience. This book proudly shares that knowledge, the intricacies of wood, fire, and smoke through a full pictorial of our legendary Fire Garden.

Fire is universal. Cooks all over the world have found fascinating ways to harness its primal power. In the pages ahead you'll find flavours and inspiration from many countries and regions of the world, including:

- ARGENTINA
- CANADA
- THE CAROLINAS
- CHINA
- CUBA
- FRANCE
- ITALY
- JAPAN
- KOREA
- LEBANON
- MEXICO
- MOROCCO
- PORTUGAL
- SPAIN
- TEXAS
- TURKEY
- VIETNAM

Wood, Fire & Smoke features a wonderful blend of practical flavours, aspirational fires, and showstopping spectacles. The lessons are real, the knowledge hard-earned, but as with all fires the stories ahead are yours. The cookbook is filled with recipes for every backyard cook, from the novice to the pro. You'll learn about wood and find tips and techniques for building and tending every type of cooking fire as well as how to harness the magical power of smoke. Even if you don't build a fire, you'll find lots of insight to up your grilling game.

WOOD PRIMER

WOOD

The hard fibrous tissue formed during the growth of trees and woody plants is the natural organic material that gives trees structural strength, the timber that gives humankind so many ingenious ways of building, crafting, and creating, and the fuel for civilization to form and flourish flavourfully. Throughout history, wood has been prized both as a building material and a reliable source of energy. Its abundant varieties and the distinctive characteristics of each are deeply understood by builders all over the globe and celebrated by cooks. We know that wood both fuels our cooking and adds flavour, so we choose it as carefully as any other ingredient in our repertoire.

TREES

In the boreal forest surrounding us, trees are a carbon-neutral, readily available renewable resource that miraculously transforms sunlight, carbon dioxide, and water into tough cellulose fibres bound by strong lignins, that is, wood. The sturdy material gives form to the tree but also conducts enough vital water that fully half the weight of freshly harvested wood is water. Within the wood of the tree are a wide variety of flammable components, some more volatile or tasty than others.

FUEL

The various natural components of wood are all flammable, but each burns in a different way. The tough fibres that form most of wood tend to ignite and smoulder slowly, thus contributing more durable heat and smoky flavour. The alcohols and compounds in the binding lignins are so volatile that they vaporize, erupt, and dissipate quickly with little effect on heat or flavour. A skilled fire cook coaxes the best from their wood. Every tree is different and thus each wood is best suited for a particular use.

HARDWOODS

Hardwood trees (known for protecting their seeds within a hard casing) are generally deciduous trees, which lose their leaves annually and grow slower, stronger, larger, and longer than their softwood cousins. Dense wood burns slowly, producing long, intensely hot fires, and as a bonus hardwood smoke tends to be pleasurably perfumed and memorably aromatic. The bulk of our cooking fires at the Inn at Bay Fortune are fuelled by a blend of locally plentiful sugar maple and white birch. We reserve apple, cherry, rock maple, yellow birch, ash, hickory, cottonwood, and alder for our many smokehouses. Our densest wood, oak, is strictly reserved for making charcoal.

SOFTWOODS

Softwood trees form seeds without protective coverings and are generally the many evergreen conifers that surround us in North America. Their fast-growing, lower density wood is saturated with flammable resins that quickly ignite and burn off, producing a bitter, acrid smoke. We don't cook with pine, spruce, or fir; they're best used as kindling to ignite prized hardwoods. Cedar is the aromatic exception, producing a delightfully gentle, fragrant smoke that's one of our favourites.

SEASONING

Wood is heavy. Half its weight at harvest is water, so strategically it's best to lose that water before starting your fire or most of the heat you manage to generate will be lost to simply making steam. Factor in the considerable effort of moving that heavy wood from the forest to the fire and ancient wisdom comes back into focus quickly: dry the tree as close as possible to where it falls but give it a hand. Bark is meant to keep water out of the tree; it keeps it in just as well. We saw our felled wood into 16-inch (40 cm) lengths, then split the blocks open to expose inner surfaces that allow natural, gradual evaporation. Neatly stacking the wood for a summer in the sun does wonders so we try to stay at least a year ahead of ourselves. We've also discovered that when it's finally time to build cooking fires, it's best to make the folks responsible for tending the fires responsible for moving the wood too. Magically we burn less.

KINDLING

It's not easy to ignite wood. The best strategy is to use a small fire to light a bigger one. We begin with kindling, our driest softwood split into small sticks. By dramatically increasing the surface area of a given volume of wood, it becomes easier to ignite the total mass. Kindling's job is to fiercely burn just long enough to ignite the fuel wood and get the fire going. It takes real effort to split a pile of kindling, so you'll quickly learn to respect your stash, using the least amount possible for each fire.

FIRE PRIMER
WOOD + OXYGEN + HEAT = FIRE

Every forest in the world is loaded with two of the three essential ingredients for a fire: plenty of wood, much of it dry, and lots of oxygen. Only when heat is added naturally or accidentally does wood ignite. Fire releases volatile gases that quickly flame away, leaving slowly burning carbon embers. It takes energy and effort to start a fire, but once it begins burning it becomes a self-sustaining system that continues burning until it eventually exhausts the available fuel.

FLAME
Flames are a mesmerizing display of the infinitely complex chemical reactions caused by the combustion processes of fire. We're drawn to their light, warmed by their heat, and inspired to cook by them. They show us that we don't have to understand life to appreciate or respect it. Fire-savvy cooks know, though, that the residues and effects of flames' spectacular chemical activity can easily overwhelm delicate ingredients. We often harness their heat but protect food from their direct touch within cast-iron pans.

EMBERS
A bed of glowing embers is the patient fire-tender's reward and generally the goal of most cooking fires. Roughly half a fire's strength quickly dissipates with the flammable gases released by the combusting wood, while the other half comes from the pure burning fuel that remains, the slow embers. Essentially pure carbon or charcoal, these glowing coals power the end of the fire. They're much easier to corral and harness than flames and offer the cook far more manageable heat.

OTHER FUELS
Today's cooks are blessed with many fuel sources, each with their own strengths and weaknesses. Gas and electricity and the conveniences of modern indoor cooking come with a clear environmental price but remain valid choices, so you'll find this book full of helpful hints for adapting flavours and ingredients to your gear.

SMOKE PRIMER
WOOD + HEAT = SMOKE

WOOD SMOKE

Smoke is a by-product of fire. Wood smoke is a combination of water vapour, various other liquids, very small solids, and a nearly infinite variety of combustion gases produced by the sustained heat of the fire. Smoke can be relatively cool or fiercely hot, but it gives far more than heat to cooks who master its primally delicious flavours.

SMOKY FLAVOUR

Wood contains a long list of organic compounds that are broken down and released by the heat of a fire. Various sugars caramelize and vaporize into an infinite variety of sweet fragrances and aromatic perfumes. Vaporous smoke carries the flavours to the surface of the food. Every tree is different, growing, burning, and smoking differently. Cooking introduces even more variables, but the basics are easily understood and the subtleties mastered through experience. Successful cooking is often a delicate dance between time and temperature; not enough or too much of either can ruin your supper.

SMOKE TEMPERATURE

As wood burns it heats through stages. Smoking begins once the wood dries past 212°F (100°C), the boiling point of water. Beyond 340°F (170°C) the smoke evolves as the fibres of the wood begin breaking down. Around 750°F (400°C) the wood blackens as the smoke tapers off. Past 1000°F (538°C) the wood fibres begin to burn, eventually reaching full combustion past 1500°F (816°C), so hot that the fire consumes the smoke before it forms. Throughout those rising temperatures, the nature and flavour of the smoke evolve dramatically as various delicious chemical reactions come and go. Since the temperatures of the wood, the fire, the smoke, and the smokehouse can all be different, it's the sustained temperature of the delicate ingredient being smoked that matters most.

SMOKE TIMING

The first smoke of a fire is dramatically white and horribly flavoured. As the fire's temperature climbs the smoke evolves, its best flavours emerge, and it becomes bluish, the distinctive hue of the sweet spot when the wood fire reaches equilibrium with its smokehouse. Since the goal of a smoking fire is not the high heat of raging flames and glowing embers, we build small fires, tend them slowly, and maximize the time the wood spends in the low-heat smoke zone.

BEYOND WOOD SMOKE

Many plants produce biomass like wood that dries and burns easily, emitting fragrant smoke worth flavouring food. Corncobs are used to smoke bacon, fresh hay to smoke cheese, tea and rice to smoke within a wok, or peat moss to smoke the barley malt for my favourite whisky. Trees also produce needles, leaves, shavings, and sawdust that can be used to smoke.

THE STAGES OF A COOKING FIRE

1. BASICS

You can build many different cooking fires from a pile of hardware basics. Cinder blocks contain a fire while offering a raised support surface. Various lengths of steel rebar are easily positioned over any fire to support the cookware of the day. Grills and grates are excellent for direct grilling or simply giving a cast-iron skillet or Dutch oven a firm place to rest.

2. BUILDING

Every fire's purpose and personality is different, so each must be built to suit, with the appropriate fuel in the chosen fire rig. Most begin the same way, though, with a careful layered alternating weave of easily ignited kindling and long-burning fuel wood. We favour the strength of a "log cabin" build and its durable coal bed, but sometimes lean a "teepee" together in a campfire ring. Our goal is not to pile on all the wood at the start but to hold back lots for later.

3. LIGHTING

There are many ways to light a fire, each as valid as the next. Matches, lighters, last night's embers, magnifying glasses, and apprentices vigorously rubbing sticks all work, but I prefer a plumber's blowtorch. It gets the job done in a hurry. Whatever your ignition source, direct it through the kindling. You'll know the wood is lit once it sustains a steady crackling sound.

4. DRAFTING

Every fire craves oxygen, so managing its vital flow is often the only way to control the works. Uncontained outdoor fires have all the air they need and are easy to light, but smaller contained smokehouse and oven fires can be tricky to get going. There are many more variables as equilibrium is established between the firebox, the fire, the oxygen feeding it through the draft, the smokehouse or oven cavity, and the smoke exiting through the chimney. The best strategy is generally open doors and full drafts to get the fire going, but once established, slowing things down considerably by restricting the same draft and flue.

5. BREAKING

To cook with fire, you must control it. Once a starter fire is established, we break it down with gloved hands, metal shovels, and iron pokers, forming it the way we want it for whatever cooking rally lies ahead. Our cooking fires often have several zones, each with a particular function as we harness their flavourful heat.

6. TENDING

Tending is the art of safely caring for a fire, giving it what *it* needs and asking it for what *you* need. A cooking fire needs careful attention, requires vigilance, and sometimes must do two things at once, giving us fuel for cooking now while simultaneously making more fuel for later. Be patient. Over time you'll develop a repertoire of techniques that help you harness the full power of your fires.

THE COOKING FIRE SPECTRUM

There are as many different cooking fires as there are cooks, each with its own purpose and personality. Over time cooks learned how to maximize their considerable efforts gathering fuel, and wood was not burned in excess. Each stage of the fire was understood, and a range of possibilities hard-earned.

When we tentatively began our culinary adventures in the wood-fired kitchen of the Inn at Bay Fortune, we naturally tried emulating the consistent heat sources we were used to, the burners, ovens, and flattops of the traditional kitchen. We know better now. We've gone further, creating an array of techniques well beyond the limits of the kitchens we knew.

There are many ways to cook with fire, each method with nuances of its own. Fire cooking can be described generally or extravagantly evocatively, but the words should be accurate, especially when they trace their roots to the traditions of a particular culture.

WOOD-FIRED: A general phrase implying the mere presence of a fire.

WOOD-ROASTED: A general phrase implying the slow temperatures of retained heat in an enclosed space, wood-fired oven, or smokehouse. Cooking within the very slow roasting temperatures next to a fire.

WOOD-GRILLED: Cooked over the direct heat of a live fire, generally the glowing embers after the flames subside.

WOOD-SMOKED: Flavoured with natural wood smoke within a smokehouse of any kind.

WOOD OVEN–BAKED: Various cooking methods performed within the magical confines of a wood-burning oven with retained heat and without a live fire.

WOOD OVEN–ROASTED: Various cooking methods performed within the magical confines of a wood-burning oven with a live fire present.

PIT-SMOKED: Food cooked over live embers, smoked only by the smoke of the meaty juices falling on the glowing coals.

PLANCHA-SEARED: Basic method using the consistent retained heat of cast iron to achieve high searing temperatures.

PLANCHA-COOKED: Basic method using the consistent retained heat of cast iron to achieve low simmering or holding temperatures.

SIDE GRILLED: Cooked slowly and indirectly next to a fire, protected from the scorching flames and direct heat.

FIRE-KISSED: Quickly cooking within the actual flames of a roaring wood fire.

BARBECUED: Various ways of cooking food with live fire and smoke, generally regionally specific.

CHARCOAL-COOKED: Various methods using the high searing heat and low smoke of well-crafted charcoal.

TOP TEN FIRE TIPS

1. **THE ZEN OF THE FIRE:** As a tool for cooking, fire offers more than heat. Within its eternal flame is a place to relax. Work hard but find the blissful moments in the flow. Cooking over a fire isn't incidental; it connects us to cooking immortal by asking us to come closer. You can't ignore a fire; you must stay focused on the task at hand. When you do, it's just you and the fire and the magical moments you make together.

2. **TAKE CONTROL:** You have the power to make a fire do what you need it to do. Respect it always but take control. Build the fire you need, then break and rebuild it with your hands and tools. Limit the fire with how much wood and oxygen you give it. Contain it for safety, ease, and efficiency. All ancient wisdom.

3. **BUILD YOUR OWN:** A world of wood, fire, and smoke requires a certain do-it-yourself mindset, the ability to imagine and rig a variety of cooking appliances on the fly. It's helpful to have a stash of cinder blocks, random rebar lengths, a library of grills, and your local metal shop on speed dial, but in the end it's the ethos to just go for it that matters.

4. **SEASON SIMPLY:** The world of fire cooking is full of bold flavours and elaborate seasoning, but a simple approach is perhaps the most powerful. While signature spice and seasoning blends have their place (there are many in this book), nothing beats just plain old salt and pepper. Pure sea salt and freshly ground black peppercorns are not only the gold standard for flavour but they're spectacularly easy!

5. **TWO-ZONE COOKING:** Building one fire to make two different heat zones is a basic fire-cooking technique. This infinitely versatile method gives the cook more options. Larger meat cuts are often best cooked by being moved from initial high searing heat to slow finishing heat. Two zones are even a chance for the fire cook to show off a bit, as multiple ingredients meet the fire at once. Delicate green vegetables can be grilled fiercely alongside slowly roasting meat and potatoes. Foods in cast-iron cookware can simmer or sear next to open grilling. Over time you'll find this an indispensable part of your style as you create your own favourite uses for two heat zones.

6. **TEMPERING AND RESTING MEAT:** Successfully cooking meat means controlling its temperature. Before cooking, tempering the meat to room temperature gives it a head start as the temperature swings ahead by shortening the perilous journey through the heat of the fire. It's difficult to properly cook the centre of cold meat without overcooking the outside. After the intense heat of the cooking fire, meat fibres need time to rest and reabsorb their own moisture. Their juices concentrate away from the hot surface, so slicing the flesh releases a pressurized torrent of vital tasty moisture. As the meat's temperature settles from high cooking heat to serving warmth, the tasty juices redistribute evenly throughout the meat.

7. **DRY BRINE:** Salting meat in advance allows the salt and the moisture within the meat to reach equilibrium. Last-second surface seasoning has its place, but most meat benefits from pre-seasoning. This gives the salt time to draw moisture from inside the meat to the surface and the meat time to draw it right back into its fibres, in effect seasoning itself from within. Genius.

8. **IRON ROCKS:** Cast-iron cookware is essential to the art and craft of wood-fired cooking. Iron's prized ability to absorb heat and radiate it evenly makes the craft of fire cooking possible. Invest in a few heavy-duty pieces of cast-iron cookware, and don't worry, they're easy to take care of.

9. **IGNORE GRILL MARKS:** The fire cook's goal is not to present a pretty pattern of perfect diamond sears but to properly care for an ingredient as it cooks. It's not necessary to constantly move the food, nor should you strive to turn it exactly once or fear budging it at all. After meat hits the grill, its fibres will eventually sear, restrict, and release from the hot metal. After the first turn, savvy fire cooks know it's best to move meat frequently to promote even cooking of its surfaces.

10. **CHARRED VERSUS BURNT:** "It's not burnt, it's charred," says every fire chef. Proximity to char often means deep, golden-brown flavour. When all else fails and you've burned something, just give it a new name and move on. Surprisingly, many ingredients in the fire cook's vast repertoire are quite tasty when burnt, ahem, charred. Winter squashes, durable vegetables with hard shells, and tough-skinned potatoes and root vegetables easily handle the heat and slip out of their charred jackets, as do multi-layered onions and leeks.

FIRE TOOLS

Every fire cook prides themselves on their kit, their hard-earned gear and tools that take the heat of the fire, that have stood the test of time. Dive into the world of wood-fired cooking and you'll find the things that work best for you. The basics below have been passed down over the ages and updated with a few modern inventions. Have a deep drawer ready, though, for stashing all the dusty gizmos and gadgets you'll also find.

SPACE FOR SAFETY: Cooking fires must be safely built well away from combustible structures or contained within properly vented fireproof masonry appliances, hearths, or ovens. A corner of your backyard can be dedicated to a homemade firepit.

FIRE WATER: Don't ignite a cooking fire until you've thought through plan B. Hook up the garden hose or ready an extinguisher. Think smart. Be safe.

HEAVY-DUTY WORK GLOVES: Gloves are essential for safety and protection as you build firepits, handle wood, and control fires. In mastering fire, your hands get hot. Heavy-duty work gloves are well insulated and protect against brief, intense heat as you move burning logs, push hot embers, and generally do what it takes by handling the fire.

CHAINSAW: A well-maintained chainsaw to limb and cut tree lengths into standard 16-inch (40 cm) blocks.

WOOD SPLITTER: A strong hydraulic wood splitter easily splits round wood blocks into smaller wedges to help them dry out and burn more efficiently. It can also be used to safely split kindling.

AXE: An axe is only needed to split kindling. A sharp axe is a safe axe.

WOOD GRILL: For a dedicated wood-fired grill you can easily upcycle an old propane or gas grill. Remove the gasworks from the largest discarded grill you can find, but keep the shell and grill assembly.

CHARCOAL GRILL: Japanese konro grills, Big Green Eggs, ceramic kamado grills, kettle drums, and hibachis are all designed to capture the intense heat of charcoal.

LOCAL STONES: Nearby stones tightly stacked into an old-fashioned campfire ring work well to safely contain a cooking fire and support the cooking surface above.

CINDER BLOCKS: You can easily dry-stack standard cinder blocks on a level fireproof surface to form an efficient firepit. The size and blocky dimensions of cinder blocks make them the ideal tool for building many different fire rigs, big or small, slow or fast.

FIREBRICKS: Masons construct ovens and hearths with fireproof firebricks built to withstand sustained intense heat. Don't use classic red bricks, which are exterior grade only and can't take the heat of a fire.

REBAR LENGTHS: With just two lengths of steel rebar or round stock you can reliably suspend a cooking grill over almost any contained cooking fire. Position rods 3 feet (1 m) or so long over the containing walls before igniting the fire. They're also useful for creating skewer supports across round grills. Ask nicely at your local metal shop: they probably have the pieces you need in their scrap pile.

GRILLS AND GRATES: Hardware stores stock standard barbecue grates to complete your homemade firepit with a direct cooking surface or resting spot for cookware.

BLOWTORCH: A standard plumber's blowtorch is the most reliable tool to quickly ignite a well-constructed cooking fire.

FIRE SHOVEL: A square-point shovel or spade works best for tending fires. It's useful both for control and for cleanup.

POKERS: You must poke the fire—it's in your genes, don't fight it. Cut a long stick, bend some metal, or buy something fancy, but be ready. It's irresistible.

CAST-IRON COOKWARE: Cast-iron cookware is essential for wood-fired cooking. Nothing matches it for durability and even heating.

STRONG METAL TONGS: Extra-long restaurant-grade metal tongs are perfect for the delicate work of the grill and the heavy-duty tasks of tending the fire.

OVENPROOF THERMOMETERS: An old-school analog thermometer can reliably help you monitor the internal cooking temperature of an enclosed wood oven.

DIGITAL THERMOMETERS: Digital precision is essential in any modern kitchen. Remote thermometers allow us to monitor slow smoking on our phones. Handheld probes give us accurate internal temperatures. Infrared thermometers measure surface temperature from a safe distance.

ASH CAN: An old-fashioned galvanized steel pan with a tight-fitting lid is perfect for weatherproofing your kit. A second one is essential for transporting spent ashes.

WOOD, FIRE & SMOKE EXPLORED

We build a myriad of cooking fires at the Inn at Bay Fortune, at least a dozen daily, each with its own purpose. Together they represent the full flavourful range of wood, fire, and smoke explored in this section.

OUR HOME HEARTH

My wife Chazz and I are blessed to have a well-worn wood-burning hearth and wood oven in our family's home. We roast, grill, and bake with it all winter long and share its bounty regularly with our friends. When I designed our house many years ago, I made the fateful last-minute decision to add a deeper foundation and build a 20,000-pound fire-breathing beast even though I had no idea how to use it. I'm glad I did because all those years of trial, error, hard-earned knowledge, and flavour gave us the confidence to wood-fire the Inn at Bay Fortune years ago.

Wood-fired cooking teaches you to never stop learning and always be your own best teacher. I've made many spectacular mistakes, filled the house with smoke multiple times, and scorched at least one priceless carpet. My family happily reminds me of the lessons learned anytime they smell a whiff of smoke, while I fondly remember the first time I grilled Wagyu beef and set the side of the house afire. That wasn't the time we called the fire department, though. Those records are sealed.

Our home fires lie dormant for the summer while I cook at the inn. In the fall I fire up the hearth for regular wood-fired meals, but not until New Year's Eve does the wood-burning oven come online. We celebrate with a night of wood-fired pizza craziness, and thus begins my annual winter cooking season. After we sleep in.

The fires of our home hearth have taught me much as a cook, husband, dad, and neighbour. I've learned intricate techniques and built broad confidence. I've found favourite flavours and created new ones. I've enjoyed the patient pace and the Zen of the flame countless times. I've learned to teach myself through simple observation, careful consideration, and relentless experimentation. The biggest lesson I've learned, though, is the power of a fire to simply bring people together. To create simple family rituals. Memorable meals. Because who's at the table matters more than what's on it.

FIREWORKS HEARTH

When we embarked on our grand wood-fired adventure at the Inn at Bay Fortune, I imagined the spectacle of the flame as much as the strength of the cooking fire. I knew we needed both, but it took years to find the best balance. We began with a spectacular showpiece, tearing off one multi-storey end of our century-old house and extending the dining rooms into a soaring space built around our brand-new wood-fired open kitchen. Every evening the Fire Brigade prepares our nightly Feast in full view of our guests, crafting a meal and creating an experience.

The FireWorks has three chimneys, three contained fires, and, as we know now, infinite uses. The wood-fired vertical smokehouse oven slowly smokes sides of salmon or slabs of pork belly or smoke-roasts lamb legs, beef ribs, or a whole turkey. The wide-open hearth deploys a dozen different cooking techniques simultaneously. Our enormous wood oven never cools down, from baking bread at dawn to roasting vegetables at dusk. We have many options, but we didn't know that at first.

My original sketches and basic design aim for the FireWorks were simple. I tried duplicating the gas-fired high-volume production systems I was used to in the professional kitchens of my career. I had a lifetime of wood-fired cooking experience at home but precisely none in a restaurant. An unconscious bar was set. After all the rapid learning and obvious drama of opening a restaurant, we found our groove. A few seasons flew by as mistakes were made, lessons learned, and our core committed team grew. Our guests loved us every step of the way, giving us confidence to keep pushing. Eventually we forgot all about normal kitchens.

Somewhere along the way we realized that we had created our own authentic wood-fired cooking style, with far more options than the gas-fired gear of a regular professional kitchen. We've mastered an ever-growing battery of techniques through the honest passion and daily effort of wood-fired cooking.

THE WOOD OVEN

Long ago cooks discovered that no matter how hot a fire is, most of its heat is lost, rising away from the food into the air above. Wood-fired ovens are designed to capture that heat, to retain it and radiate it back to the food, even in the complete absence of a fire. The mouth of the oven ingeniously allows vital oxygen to reach the active fire while simultaneously allowing smoke to escape and food to come and go.

Baking naturally fermented bread in a wood-fired oven is one of the highest achievements of the culinary arts. The legendary connection our baker has with their oven is a beautiful dance of long tradition, instinctive craft, and deeply personal art. Every day is different. There's no manual, there are infinite variables, and you're baking with yesterday's heat.

Pizzas are baked quickly from the heat of a live fire in the oven, but bread burns near a fire, so we bake it after the fire dies down. The floor and domed cavity of our masonry wood oven are constructed of special fireproof bricks. Above the ceiling are several tons of heat-retaining sand. Every spring when we first fire the oven for the season it takes a full week to fully heat that thermal mass. Once it's hot, though, it's easy to maintain its consistent even heat with daily fires.

We bake bread first thing in the morning with the low retained heat of the wood oven but end the day with an active fire for dinner service. The intense high heat of that contained fire is an essential part of how we craft our tasting menus' intricate flavours. As our guests leave, we stoke the fire, bank it for the night, and the cycle begins yet again.

THE BEAST

Once upon a time there was an expensive restaurant on an island bay. Then one day the whole world got sick and the restaurant had to change, so it became a take-out joint, and the Beast was born. Taming it is another story.

Our team spent the 2020 season sharing a picnic for the ages with our Atlantic Bubble community. Brightly coloured picnic tables on the front lawn became our dining room, and we poured our culinary passion into filling our daily picnic basket with honest flavours. Take-out could only mean one thing: barbecue, as authentic as could be, which meant the holy trio of smoked pork ribs, homemade sausage, and, fatefully, tender brisket. I remembered the old water tank behind the barn, and after a reread of the bible, Aaron Franklin's classic *Franklin Barbecue*, and a week at our local custom metal shop, we had a freshly painted Southern-style offset pit smoker. I even had an old trophy head for the front. It was a thing of beauty, but we had no idea how to use it yet.

The Beast was born of necessity. Taming it became our mission. Chef Chris Gibb led the way, Vulcan mind locking himself to the soul of its fire until he mastered it. Then he taught the rest of us, and a legend was born: Beast Brisket. The intricate challenge of transforming this tough beef cut into tender, succulent magic has consumed us ever since.

If grilling a hamburger is kindergarten, then wood-smoking a brisket is a PhD. No matter the cooking method, the cut is perhaps the single most difficult to prepare. Breast meat is riddled with tough connective tissue that will dissolve only after long, patient heating, but it's also full of beefy moisture that evaporates easily. Hours of effort can be destroyed in minutes. Fortunately, our Beast can dance!

Our Picnic Days were a hit, kept our team going, and saved our business. We've kept smoking brisket since then, not just as a reminder of those days but because we discovered one of the highest orders of our wood-fired craft. We tamed our beast.

THE FIRE HOUSE

The Fire House is the headquarters of the Fire Garden. Its bright red roof keeps dry everything we need to build every form of fire known to humans: hardwood, softwood, fruitwood, fuel wood, smoking wood, kindling, charcoal, a potato gun, bright red beer cooler, and an ever-growing collection of gizmos, gadgets, and fire tools.

Mastering fire requires your hands, your presence, and lots of tools, as many as you can dream up. Start with the basics: a strong axe, heavy-duty work gloves, extra-long tongs, a tough metal spatula preferably with a cool wood handle, a flat-bottomed spade, a metal pail with a tight-fitting lid, and a plumber's blowtorch. Over time you'll understand your needs and start to create your own inventions. Before you know it you'll be on a first-name basis with the team at your local metal shop and need a fancy red-roofed shed for your collection of gear and wood.

We prize wood like any other ingredient in our pantry, giving it a place to stay dry and organized. Dry wood ignites easily, burns hotter, and creates the best smoke. In our smokehouses we smoulder as many types of fragrant local wood as we can get our hands on. Rock maple, sugar maple, yellow birch, white birch, apple, cherry, cottonwood, cedar, alder, even fresh hay, autumn leaves, and cedar shavings all have their spot.

When it rains, the Fire House hosts a tasting station under its cheerful awning. Our guests enjoy mingling while imagining uses for the bizarre array of medieval tools we've collected. Rain or shine, though, we're ready, because when the sun comes back there's always another fire to light.

THE FIRE ALTAR TACO AND HOT SAUCE BAR

We have many fire altars at the Inn at Bay Fortune but only one with a taco and hot sauce bar. When you make as many cooking fires as we do, you'll quickly realize that cooking on the ground has its limitations. It's okay occasionally, but not day after day. A waist-high wood cooking fire is the dream, so we hauled in huge sandstone boulders and build fires on top of them daily. Fire altars.

Our Fire Garden guests come and go, so our fires must sustain their readiness for hours. To properly craft our tacos, we build a three-zone fire with low heat for toasting our handmade tortillas, high heat to cook whatever we're stuffing them with, and a nursery for making embers so we don't fall behind. This Fire Station is one of our most advanced, but only here do our guests get to add their own heat.

In our basement SkunkWorks we preserve, ferment, hydrate, dehydrate, rehydrate, and generally make flavourful magic with our own farm-fresh harvest and various other odd ingredients. All the world's great hot sauces are patiently fermented for flavour, so every year we carefully preserve our chili pepper harvest. The array of flavoursome spicy hot sauces we create become next year's hot sauce bar.

Tacos are a fun way to serve an array of spectacular farm-fresh vegetables and varied proteins from our island's many farmers. They're not pretentious, just easy and delicious, so our guests tend to relax and try new things. Many a tentative palate has enjoyed its first taste of goat, alpaca, beef heart, or eel at the Fire Altar, but even an experienced palate can still get schooled.

On our culinary farm we grow medium-heat chili peppers that thrive in our climate zone, prizing their intense aromatic flavours over the mind-numbing spiciness of tropical plants. Our hot sauces are gloriously flavourful and plenty spicy, but some free spirit always wants more, so of course our crafty chefs are ready. The under-the-table bottle is loaded with come-from-away chili heat dialled up to the legal max. We warn them, but they don't listen.

THE ASADOR SHED

One of the biggest challenges in the world of wood-fired cooking is preparing a whole animal. No matter the species—lamb, goat, alpaca, pig, even steer—the fire cook has to successfully manhandle hundreds of pounds of meat, deal with an array of different cuts each with its own cooking needs, and build a fire big enough to get the job done.

An asador is a tool, a cook, and an occasion. The large metal frame that supports a whole animal over the fire, the cook who tends the meat, and the automatic party that breaks out are all part of Argentinean tradition. In the Fire Garden we pay homage to South American fire culture as we slowly roast our local meats.

As with so many fire-cooking techniques, an asador requires patience. It can take an entire day to cook a whole animal and the fire must be slowly dialed in the whole time. If the fire is too hot, the surface of the flesh will char and burn long before the centre cooks through. The secret is to offset the asador frame from the direct heat of the fire, positioning it next to but not above the embers. We've even added a shed to help contain the fire.

Rain doesn't stop the Fire Brigade, so on misty days the roof above our asador fire keeps the works dry and slowly blazing. Rain or shine, the shed's walls and ceiling corral the fire, dramatically increasing its efficiency by directing the heat and smoke towards the slowly roasting meat.

Our asador shed is always the centre of attention. Roasting an entire animal is an implicit invitation to relax and enjoy the party. It's a primal tradition to gather around the fire to swap stories and flavours.

OYSTER ROCK

We love oysters at the Inn at Bay Fortune. We're on an island legendary for them, blessed with a bayful out front, shuck tens of thousands annually, and serve almost all of them straight up raw. We really don't like cooking our local oysters because their delicate briny flavours are so easily lost to the heat of a fire. We have figured out a way, though.

Sometimes you just must get outside and get a fire going to get what you want. Every day on Oyster Rock we build a large hardwood fire, wait patiently for a thick, glowing bed of embers, and then shuck fresh oysters, carefully retaining their juices in their level shells. And then our special touch.

Lovage has long been one of my favourite herbs. I love the deep green of its broad leaves, its celery-like perfume, and the easy neutrality of its flavour. We purée it into a shockingly green and flavourful compound butter and spoon some on every oyster before it's nestled in the hot embers. Tasty butter made with lovage—we call it Love Butter because we're that kind of hotel.

Oysters resting in the embers of a fire quickly absorb heat through their shells. Their juices briefly protect them as they bubble, lightly poaching as green butter bathes them with subtle yet rich complementary flavour. It doesn't take long for all this to happen, just a minute or so until just barely warmed through, and they must be enjoyed fresh from the fire to best appreciate their glory.

Oyster Rock represents our very best. Oysters from the bay out front roasting in the embers of a warm fire on a sunny summer day. Hungry travellers and passionate cooks with awesome local ingredients drawn to the heat of the fire. Stories and flavours together.

THE WINTER AND
SUMMER SMOKEHOUSES

I love smoking salmon. I love choosing from a dozen different aromatic woods and tasting how easily the rich, fatty fish absorbs the subtleties of a particular wood's smoke. I love learning by doing, and I love how every smokehouse has its own unique personality. Most of all I treasure how many of our guests change their minds and fall in love with smoked salmon after trying ours.

We begin with the very best salmon we can find. Sustainable Blue is our favourite East Coast choice. The company raises fish in a land-based closed-loop, zero-effluent organic system that mimics nature. The fish grow slowly and are spectacularly flavourful. We cure the sides with sea salt, brown sugar, and our signature Bay Spice for a few days, patiently seasoning the flesh before smoking it.

Salmon is much more delicate than the tough fibrous meats we smoke. The fish's vital moisture is easily lost to the high heat of a fire, so our smokehouses are designed to operate at much lower temperatures. A small smouldering fire in an offset firebox forces the smoke to travel a length of cooling pipe before it enters the smokehouse. Our summer smokehouse has an extra-long pipe to cool the smoke as much as possible and is insulated against the exterior summer heat.

Even with all our cooling efforts, though, our signature salmon is still technically hot-smoked, spending 6 to 8 hours at a smoky 150°F (65°C), lightly firming the flesh without drying it out. Its succulent texture is very different from traditional lox-style smoked salmon.

Most of our salmon is cold-smoked in an actual refrigerator that keeps the fish well below cooking temperatures. I prefer not to run a power cord to my smokehouses, though, so I wait for winter to cold-smoke salmon and let Mother Nature cool the works for me to 50°F (10°C) or so. In the depths of winter, I can smoke for days.

CHARCOAL STREET

Of the many fires we build daily, perhaps none get as hot as our charcoal fires. We sear an array of proteins and vegetables daily at our Charcoal Street station over our own homemade lump charcoal. We bake wood at sub-combustion temperatures in the absence of oxygen to craft the black carbon residue used to cook so many of the world's great street foods.

Cities don't produce fuel, they import it. Historically, heavy wood was often found a great distance from where it was needed. Making charcoal dramatically lightens the weight of the wood while preserving its carbon heat potential. It's an excellent cooking fuel, igniting easily and burning fiercely hot.

Very dense local oak is our first choice for making charcoal, producing the longest- and hottest-burning coals. We tightly pack a small barrel with oak, seal it tightly, sit it on a strong frame, and cover it with a larger barrel, leaving an airspace between the two. A steady fire is built under the inner barrel, its heat contained by the outer barrel, and after hours of heating, the wood within releases its moisture and volatile gases. Three small holes drilled in the bottom of the barrel allow the pressurized gases to escape and ignite spectacularly. For an hour or so as the wood finishes baking, the barrel resembles a rocket ship straining to launch. The spectacle proves that the inner barrel is pressurized enough to keep oxygen away from the wood so it doesn't burn.

Charcoal gets extremely hot, so it's excellent for instantly searing small portions of meat or fish. Since the woodsmoke is long gone, the coals produce no flavour of their own. Instead, juices falling from the food above burst into flame, producing a distinctive smoke.

Charcoal briquettes are made from sawdust and binding agents. They burn lower and slower than lump charcoal, so they're best reserved for cooking large cuts of meat or whole fowl.

THE KONRO GRILL

We burn exclusively local woods in the Fire Garden, but we do make one exception for the world's very best charcoal. Our konro grill is authentically fuelled with binchotan charcoal from the mountains of Japan. The ancient artisanal process produces a fuel from extremely dense ubame oak that's more like brittle china than typical soft charcoal.

A konro is a portable rectangular grill created to cook with white-hot binchotan. Artisans carve the grill from a solid block of diatomaceous earth, the fossilized remains of ancient plankton and algae. This concrete-like material excels at containing and insulating the charcoal's high heat. Its long, narrow shape is perfect for holding rows of searing skewers.

We make our own charcoal in the Fire Garden, so naturally we're a bit obsessed with the stuff. Our own local oak charcoal is the best we've ever crafted, but it will never be as good as binchotan. The fiercest heat of the day is always in the konro, literal white heat.

Binchotan ignites slowly, but once it's ripping, the coals turn white and begin glowing from within with infrared radiant heat. Most fires produce heat through convection, the movement of hot air, while the konro's radiant heat is far hotter, more consistent, and nearly instantaneous. The intense heat sears the surface of the protein so quickly that it doesn't have a chance to dry out.

We really enjoy cooking on our konro and try hard to share flavours authentic to the gear. We love the insane heat, the tasty results, and the living, breathing connection we've built with the charcoal artisans and street food artists of Japan.

THE ROTISSERIE RIG

Rotisserie, or spit-roasting, is a style of cooking characterized by large cuts of meat skewered on a long metal rod, slowly rotating and patiently roasting in front of a smoky fire. The slow, controlled rotation allows the meat to cook evenly while continually basting in its own juices. Slowly rotating meat doesn't lose its essential juices; the flavourful moisture clings to the surface instead of falling away. The results are spectacularly delicious.

The rotisserie spit is offset from the direct heat of the fire to prevent burning during the long cooking time. The spit can also be adjusted up or down to calibrate the nearby heat. The offset heat from a steady fire over a glowing bed of coals works best, so we build an open weave, laying split logs alternately atop each other. To keep the spit turning, we rely on apprentices. Their job is to keep the long extension cord plugged in.

We can fit six big yard birds on the spit, slowly cooking their tough meat until it eventually tenderizes. We love wrapping the belly of a freshly butchered pig around its loin to create a classic porchetta. We've had success with larger root vegetables too. Celery root comes alive on the spit.

Our rotisserie rig in the Fire Garden is engineered to handle an entire pig. The weight of the beast must be perfectly balanced around the spit or the slowly turning motor will overheat. An ingenious system of counterweights centres the weight and keeps the rod turning evenly. Dry-stacked cinder blocks and a steel shed roof contain the smoky heat, adding efficiency to the works.

A rotisserie is patient. Hours of slow rotation remind us that life has its own pace and we're at our best when we go with the flow.

THE BIG GREEN EGGS

This is not an endorsement, but I suspect the folks at Big Green Egg will be happy to read my words, because to me my battery of Big Green Eggs is far more than a collection of flawless cooking gear. In my life they were first, they started the fire. They're part of me now.

Big Green Egg is a brand name for a type of Japanese-style kamado grill often known as kettle grills. They are characterized by their colourful egg shape and ease of use. They're made of high-tech ceramic that easily contains their heat. Temperature control is as simple as adjusting the lower air vent and the upper smoke vent. In minutes I can be steakhouse-searing a juicy ribeye at high heat or embarking on an hours-long low-heat smoking adventure.

A cooking fire burning down to embers in an improvised firepit is one thing; spending lots of money on gear to recreate a firepit is quite another. I've had limited success with gas grills. They work but they're not inspiring. I had a giant expensive one once, but now all that's left are its heavy-duty grates. My first Egg is twenty years old and still going strong.

Kamado grills are designed for charcoal, but I discovered long ago that they also work well with a wood fire. My large Egg was my go-to back deck winter cooker for many years before we bought the inn. Now we have four, a versatile small, medium, and large trio in the Fire Garden and the biggest one on our back deck east of Montreal.

My Egg was the first gear that pulled me out of the inside kitchen into the realm of outdoor possibility. While I shared years of deliciousness, it gave me the confidence to grow, push the boundaries, stay outside, and see what other rigs I can dream up!

THE COPPER DOME

The Copper Dome is a historic wood-fired oven. Thirty years ago, the folks at Speerville Flour Mills in New Brunswick built it on a trailer and started hauling it to every granola festival on the East Coast. I remember bumping into them once or twice, never imagining that someday this gleaming masterpiece might be ours. After changing owners and spending a few years in a dusty Halifax garage, it found its way to the inn's Fire Garden, where it has come alive once again.

The Copper Dome is best for high-heat roasting and speedy pizza baking, not slow bread baking. Unlike our FireWorks oven it has very little thermal mass above the oven cavity, so once the fire dies down it doesn't retain the heat needed to cook. Instead, we cook quickly with the fire banked to one side. When pizzas are on the menu, we even add a small piece of split kindling with each bake. It quickly lights afire, licking the ceiling with flames and browning the top of the pizza.

We are a vegetable-forward restaurant, so naturally we roast bone marrow daily in the Copper Dome. Splitting a beef leg bone in half to expose the fatty marrow within is our favourite play. Roasting elevates the rich beefy flavour, and then we simply whisk it into a dressing with homemade mustard and vinegar. Bone marrow mustard dressing awaiting a roasted vegetable. A little bit goes a long way. Our culinary farm gives us a daily vegetable harvest of incredible diversity, almost all of which can be successfully prepared in the wood oven. A durable root vegetable, a semi-firm squash, a juicy tomato, and a delicate green sprout all require different cooking methods, but everything tastes good lightly tossed with bone marrow dressing!

WOOD CANDLES

A classic wood candle is the most ingenious cooking fire I know how to make. It's portable, lightweight, ignites easily, burns for hours, and produces wildly efficient heat, all while firmly supporting a pan.

The Swedish army is credited with creating the first wood candles during the Thirty Years' War in the 1600s. The Swedes are legendary masters of forest craft and understood instinctively all the logistical challenges of feeding an army. To be nimble they knew they couldn't march with their fuel source, nor could they expect to find extravagant amounts of wood on the way. They needed efficiency, so that's what they invented.

Wood fires are generally very inefficient; most of their heat is lost long before they're ready for cooking. You can cook only so much food with an armload of wood, so naturally maximizing yield is part of the play. That's the genius of the wood candle: it's efficient and very little heat goes to waste.

Choose a standard 16-inch (40 cm) block of seasoned hardwood, the wider the better. Fire up your chainsaw and make two perpendicular cuts through the centre but not to the bottom, leaving 6 inches (15 cm) or so at the bottom to hold the works together. Stuff the centre with dry tinder and light it up. Then stand back and marvel at your (or the Swedes') cleverness.

The log ignites easily and burns slowly from the inside out, leaving stable supports for a large pan on top. Instead of waiting for a bed of coals, you'll find yourself cooking in just a few minutes, and you'll enjoy a solid hour of cooking time. The fire is off the ground, and in winter snow that's a lifeline.

Wood candles are also a showstopping spectacle. Expect a crowd to gather around, lots of oohs and aahs, and be ready to show them how to make their own.

THE CAMPFIRE

The best fires are not for cooking. Instead we build them for warmth and fellowship. Few things draw humans together so powerfully as a crackling campfire. A friendly fire is a literal reminder of humanity's strength and how far we've come together.

Humans build fires, and long ago we learned to harness their merry warmth and cooking potential. Anthropologists believe that the control of fire and the way heat makes meat more edible gave early peoples the ready protein they needed to launch humankind. Today we're still drawn to the flickering flames.

Towards the evening's end as our guests enjoy the FireWorks Feast, a roaring campfire erupts on the front lawn. We reserve local tamarack for our non-cooking campfires. This resinous softwood is so full of oil that it snaps and crackles more brightly than any other wood we burn. We're careful to stack lots of it nearby and leave a few solid pokers lying around too. A natural rhythm tends to emerge as everyone indulges their primal instincts, poking and stoking the fire.

Many fancy restaurants like ours end the evening with a mignardise, a sweet taste or two arriving after dessert, an invitation to linger. Our surprise treat is a homemade marshmallow from the imagination of our pastry chef. Our guests leave their tables with the day's flavour skewered on a long stick and head straight for the flames.

A campfire is an invitation, an implicit request to join the fun. As the meal finishes, the fire's beckoning flames draw our guests to an ecumenical gathering. They sit, they snuggle, they chat, and they linger into the wee hours with millions of years of history at their backs.

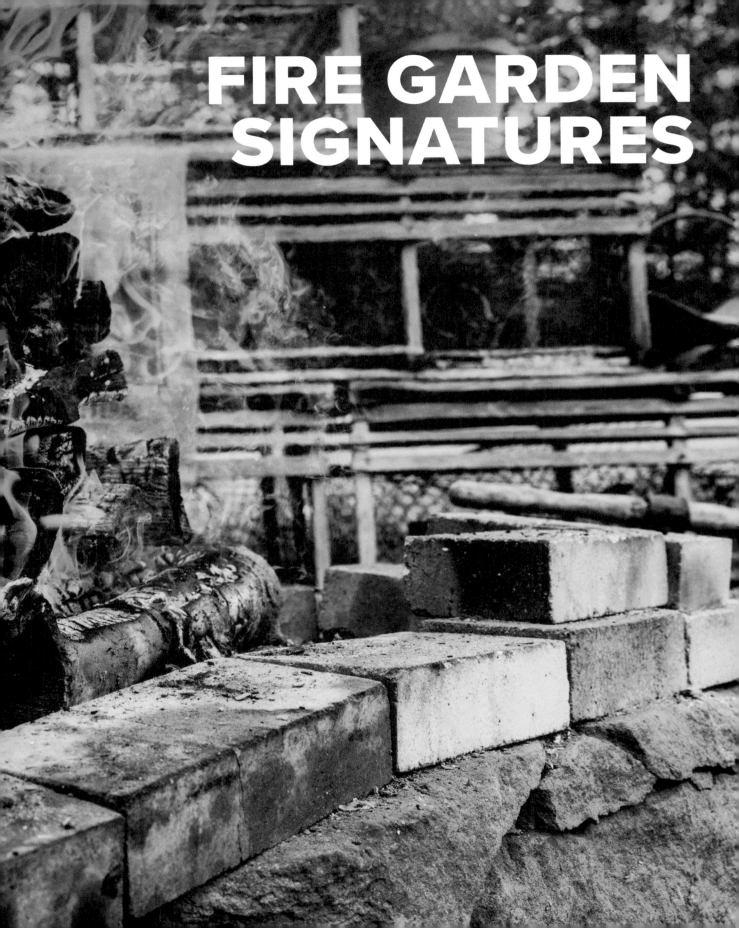

FIRE GARDEN
SIGNATURES

CEDAR-SMOKED OYSTERS WITH SPRUCE TIP BUTTER

Fresh briny oysters lightly smoked with surprisingly fragrant cedar, gently cooked with butter infused with tender spruce tips foraged from the trees' spring growth.

MAKE THE SPRUCE TIP BUTTER

Bring a medium pot of lightly salted water to a full boil, then adjust the heat to maintain a steady simmer. Fill a large bowl with the coldest water your taps can muster.

Working quickly, plunge the spruce tips into the simmering water, stirring and swirling as they immediately brighten and wilt, just 10 seconds or so. Drain through a mesh strainer or colander without pressing. Quickly transfer the wet shoots to the cold water, swirling until cool, a minute or so. Drain again without pressing. Transfer the wet spruce tips to a high-speed blender. Add the 2 tablespoons (30 mL) cold water. Purée, scraping down the sides once or twice, until bright green and thoroughly smooth. Transfer to a small bowl and refrigerate, uncovered, until cold. Reserve the blender.

Add the butter to the blender. Purée the butter, scraping down the sides once or twice, until smooth. Add the chilled spruce tip purée and continue processing until smooth. Store in a resealable container in the fridge for up to 1 month or in the freezer for up to 6 months.

BUILD A FIRE AND SOAK THE CEDAR

Build and tend a wood or charcoal fire in a Big Green Egg or other ceramic kamado-style grill, until it subsides into a thick bed of glowing hot coals. Remove the grill grate and reserve for the oysters.

Soak the cedar shavings or chips in water for a few minutes, then drain.

READY THE OYSTERS

Carefully shuck the oysters, taking special care not to spill their tasty brine. Fill the grill grate with oysters, placing them as level as possible, steadying between the bars and nestling against each other. Top each oyster with a teaspoon or so of spruce tip butter.

CEDAR-SMOKE THE OYSTERS

Open the lid of the grill. Evenly sprinkle the moist cedar shavings over the coal bed. Place the oyster-laden grill grate in position. Immediately close the lid and the top and bottom vents. Patiently wait for 3 minutes while the oysters lightly poach in their own juices surrounded by the fragrant cedar smoke. Carefully open the lid and check the oysters: they're done when their juices begin gently simmering at the edges and they plump. Carefully remove the grate and let the oysters rest a moment or two until cool enough to slurp. Repeat with the remaining oysters.

SERVES 8 TO 12

SPECIAL EQUIPMENT NEEDED: Big Green Egg or other ceramic kamado-style grill; oyster shucking knives; extra-long metal tongs; heavy-duty work gloves

SPRUCE TIP BUTTER

1 cup (250 mL) freshly foraged spruce tips

2 tablespoons (30 mL) cold water

1 cup (250 mL) butter, at room temperature

2 quarts (2 L) moist cedar shavings or cedar chips

4 dozen impeccably fresh Prince Edward Island oysters, or your favourite variety, from a well-connected fishmonger

CEDAR SMOKING
Traditional Smoking Method

Cedar is the only softwood we use at the inn for smoking. Unlike hardwoods, softwoods such as pine, spruce, and fir are very resinous, producing clouds of acrid, bitter smoke. Somehow, though, the smoke of fragrant cedar is distinctively perfumed and delicious. Cedar slabs smoulder for hours in our smokehouses, and their shavings impart finishing flavours in minutes.

SAFETY NOTE: A thicker oyster shell forgotten over the fire by a distracted cook will eventually dry out and may crack or explode. It's not particularly dangerous, but it is sudden and surprising, and easily avoided by not overcooking the oysters.

FLAMBADOU-ROASTED OYSTERS
WITH BAY SPICE SPRINKLE AND RED ONION DILL RELISH

A spectacular party trick and a memorably flavourful way to lightly cook oysters with true medieval flair. Flaming hot droplets of rendered beef fat sizzling with a sprinkle of our aromatic signature spice, finished with a bright herbaceous relish.

MAKE THE RED ONION DILL RELISH

Measure the red wine vinegar, sugar, hot sauce, and salt into a medium saucepan. Bring to a full boil over medium-high heat. Stir in the red onion and continue cooking until the mixture simmers yet again. Remove from the heat. Cover tightly with a lid and let rest for 20 minutes. Transfer the relish to a resealable container, tightly seal, and refrigerate until thoroughly chilled, at least an hour or overnight. Just before serving, stir in the minced dill.

BUILD A FIRE

Build and tend an active fire in your firepit, bringing to high heat with live flame and a growing bed of glowing hot coals. Position the cup end of the flambadou in the hottest part of the fire, nestled directly in the coals. Fiercely preheat until the iron is glowing red.

SHUCK THE OYSTERS

Away from the fire, carefully shuck the oysters, taking special care not to spill their tasty brine. Invert the top shells onto a large fireproof surface. Steady the oyster-filled half shells against the accumulating top shells. Lightly sprinkle each oyster with a pinch of bay spice.

ROAST THE OYSTERS

Carefully remove the flambadou from the fire and drop a large chunk of fat into it. The fat will immediately begin to render and drip through the lower hole. Hold near the fire to ignite the steady stream, then position the flambadou 8 inches (20 cm) or so above the oysters. Carefully direct a few of the flaming droplets over each oyster, allowing the heat to lightly cook and flavour them. Serve with a small dollop of red onion dill relish. Garnish with the reserved dill sprigs.

SERVES 8 TO 12

SPECIAL EQUIPMENT NEEDED:
flambadou (see note below); heavy-duty work gloves

RED ONION DILL RELISH

½ cup (125 mL) red wine vinegar

½ cup (125 mL) sugar

1 teaspoon (5 mL) of your favourite hot sauce

¼ teaspoon (1 mL) sea salt

1 large red onion, finely minced

Leaves and tender stems from 1 large bunch of fresh dill, minced, a few sprigs reserved for garnish

FLAMING OYSTERS

4 dozen impeccably fresh Prince Edward Island oysters, or your favourite variety, from a well-connected fishmonger

2 tablespoons (30 mL) Bay Spice (page 256) or Old Bay seasoning, chili powder, curry powder, or your favourite spice blend

A 4-ounce (115 g) chunk of pure beef or pork fat, cut into several large chunks

FLAMBADOU
Medieval Kitchen Tool

An inverted cone-shaped steel cooking tool with a tiny hole in the bottom designed to hold slowly rendering chunks of fat over roasting meat, basting it with flavourful drips. To spectacularly roast oysters, the cone is heated in the embers of a fire until glowing. A steady stream of flaming droplets emerges from the bottom, igniting instantly before searing the surface of the oyster below.

EMBER-ROASTED OYSTERS WITH LOVE BUTTER

These oysters are legendary. Every day this signature recipe kicks off Oyster Hour in our Fire Garden at the inn. The ancient cooking technique of ember roasting, capturing the last heat of a hardwood fire, gently poaches the oysters, cooking them in their own juices with aromatic Love Butter just until firm yet still tender. The bright green compound butter is named for lovage, a distinctive celery-flavoured herb grown on our culinary farm. Oysters are always a party, especially when they bring us together around a fire.

SERVES 8 TO 12

SPECIAL EQUIPMENT NEEDED: oyster shucking knives; fire shovel; extra-long metal tongs; heavy-duty work gloves

LOVE BUTTER
1 cup (250 mL) fresh lovage leaves
2 tablespoons (30 mL) cold water
1 cup (250 mL) butter, at room temperature

4 dozen impeccably fresh Prince Edward Island oysters, or your favourite variety, from a well-connected fishmonger

MAKE THE LOVE BUTTER

Bring a medium pot of lightly salted water to a full boil, then adjust the heat to maintain a steady simmer. Fill a large bowl with the coldest water your taps can muster.

Working quickly, plunge the lovage leaves into the simmering water, stirring and swirling as they immediately brighten and wilt, just 10 seconds or so. Drain through a mesh strainer or colander without pressing. Quickly transfer the wet leaves to the cold water, swirling until cool, a minute or so. Drain again without pressing. Transfer the wet leaves to a blender. Add the 2 tablespoons (30 mL) cold water. Purée, scraping down the sides once or twice, until bright green and thoroughly smooth. Transfer to a small bowl and refrigerate, uncovered, until cold. Reserve the blender.

Add the butter to the blender or a food processor. Purée the butter, scraping down the sides once or twice, until smooth. Add the chilled lovage purée and continue processing until smooth. Store in a resealable container in the fridge for up to 1 month or in the freezer for up to 6 months.

BUILD A FIRE

Build and tend a large fire in your firepit, bringing to a pile of glowing hot coals. Using a fire shovel, form the hot coals into a thick bed of embers about 2-foot (60 cm) square. Alternatively, light your charcoal grill or fire up your gas grill to its highest setting.

READY THE OYSTERS

Carefully shuck the oysters, taking special care not to spill their tasty brine. Invert the top shells onto a serving platter or baking sheet. Steady the full oyster-filled half shells against the accumulating top shells. Scrape some of the love butter into soft shards. Top each oyster with a teaspoon or so.

Recipe continues

EMBER-ROAST THE OYSTERS

Grasp the edge of a shell with extra-long tongs and nestle the oyster firmly into the embers. Repeat until the first dozen oysters are cooking. Take vigil as the juices and melted butter mingle, the oysters just barely poaching, 1 to 2 minutes. They're done when the juices begin gently simmering at the edges and the oysters visibly plump. Any longer and they will shrivel, toughen, and dry out. Carefully remove the oysters from the coals and rest them again on the top shells until cool enough to slurp. Repeat with the remaining oysters.

EMBER ROASTING
Traditional Cooking Method

Cooking directly on or in the ash-free and smoke-free glowing embers of a late-stage hardwood fire.

SAFETY NOTE: A thicker oyster shell forgotten in the fire by a distracted cook will eventually dry out and may crack or explode. It's not particularly dangerous, but it is sudden and surprising, and easily avoided by not overcooking the oysters.

YAKITORI CHICKEN SKEWERS WITH TARE SAUCE AND NORI SHICHIMI

The classic street food of Japan: impeccable ingredients elevated with devoted attention to every detail. Simple skewers of chicken seared over the intense heat of binchotan, the world's very best charcoal, contained in a classic konro grill, dipped in sweet soy-based tare sauce, glazed over the charcoal, then enjoyed immediately with a sprinkle of authentic seven-spice shichimi. (In Japan, yakitori masters meticulously butcher chicken into dozens of individual small muscles.)

MAKE THE NORI SHICHIMI

In a small skillet over medium-high heat, toast the white and black sesame seeds, stirring frequently, until fragrant and lightly coloured. Transfer to a small bowl, then add the ground nori, gochugaru, yuzu peel, poppy seeds, and ginger. Mix well. Reserve or store in a small resealable container at room temperature for up to 1 month.

MAKE THE TARE SAUCE

Preheat the oven to 425°F (220°C). Turn on the convection fan if you have one.

Pile the green onions and ginger slices in the centre of a roasting pan. Cover with the chicken parts. Roast, uncovered, until the chicken is golden brown and caramelized, 30 minutes or so. Carefully pour off accumulated fat, reserving for another use. Transfer the chicken, green onions, and ginger to a large saucepan. Pour the water into the roasting pan and stir to dissolve all the browned bits. Pour into the saucepan. Add the sake, soy sauce, mirin, and sugar. Bring to a slow, steady simmer, cover tightly, and cook until thickened and deeply infused with colour and flavour, 45 minutes. Remove the lid, increase the heat, and quickly reduce the sauce, thickening it to 2 cups (500 mL) or so. Remove from the heat and let sit until cool enough to handle. Pour the sauce through a fine-mesh strainer into a heatproof container. Refrigerate until cold and firm. Before using, remove any fat that congeals on the surface.

PREP THE CHICKEN SKEWERS

Thread the meat onto the skewers, alternating chicken pieces with green onion. Trim away any dangly chicken bits to prevent charring.

Recipe continues

MAKES 12 SKEWERS, SERVES 4 TO 6

SPECIAL EQUIPMENT NEEDED: konro, hibachi, or ceramic kamado-style grill; binchotan charcoal; 12 bamboo skewers, soaked in water overnight, or metal skewers; deep narrow tare pot (optional)

NORI SHICHIMI (MAKES ABOUT 1 CUP/ 250 ML)

2 tablespoons (30 mL) white sesame seeds

2 tablespoons (30 mL) black sesame seeds

1 standard 8-inch (20 cm) square sheet nori, ground into a powder

¼ cup (60 mL) gochugaru

1 tablespoon (15 mL) dried yuzu peel or chenpi (dried orange peel)

1 tablespoon (15 mL) poppy seeds

1 tablespoon (15 mL) ground ginger

TARE SAUCE (MAKES ABOUT 2 CUPS/ 500 ML)

1 bunch of green onions

6 ounces (170 g) unpeeled fresh ginger, washed, thinly sliced

1 pound (450 g) skin-on, bone-in chicken parts (necks, backs, carcass bones, or wings)

1 cup (250 mL) water

2 cups (500 mL) sake

2 cups (500 mL) soy sauce

1 cup (250 mL) mirin

1 cup (250 mL) sugar

YAKITORI CHICKEN SKEWERS

1½ pounds (675 g) boneless chicken (thigh or breast meat, with or without the skin, wings with wingtips removed, or livers), cut into even 1½-inch (4 cm) pieces

6 green onions, cut into 2-inch (5 cm) lengths

BUILD A FIRE

Fill a fire basket with binchotan charcoal and ignite within the roaring flames of an active fire or within a charcoal chimney. Build a tightly packed single-layer charcoal fire in a konro or other charcoal grill. Alternatively, build a lump charcoal fire in a hibachi, kamado, or backyard charcoal grill. Cover carefully with a second layer of coals. Vigorously fan the coals to help fully ignite the charcoal. Tend to a glowing bed of fiercely hot glowing white coals. The charcoal will progress through three distinct phases, from cold and black through surface ignition (indicated by an even feathery grey coat), before full ignition eventually penetrates to the centre and it begins glowing cherry red from within. If necessary, position skewer supports over the coals.

GRILL THE CHICKEN SKEWERS

Transfer the tare sauce to a traditional tare pot or small saucepan and bring to a bare simmer to one side of the fire. Vigorously fan the coals to increase their searing heat. Place the chicken skewers directly on the konro edges or skewer supports. Cook the chicken like a human-powered rotisserie, turning and tending constantly, searing the meat until golden brown, tender, juicy, and nearly fully cooked, 5 minutes or so.

Remove the skewers from the heat, dip into the tare sauce, return to the heat, and glaze, turning and tending constantly, a minute or so more. Dip and grill once or twice more, carefully glazing the chicken without scorching or burning. Remove from the heat, dip once more in the tare sauce, sprinkle generously with lots of nori shichimi, and serve immediately.

Briefly return any leftover tare sauce to a simmer, tightly cover, and refrigerate for regular use and replenishment or freeze in an airtight container for up to 6 months to begin your next batch—see Perpetual Tare: Ancient Cooking Method, page 70.

BINCHOTAN
Artisanal Fuel Source

Considered the world's best charcoal, this traditional fuel has been crafted by Japanese artisans for thousands of years from the country's native white oak. It burns at a very high temperature for an extended time and is the preferred fuel for the konro grill, producing intense infrared heat and glowing white.

APPLE CHICKEN SKEWERS WITH MULLED CIDER TARE SAUCE AND SEVEN-SPICE SPRINKLE

Our version of classic yakitori, Japan's popular street food, each element elevated with our own Prince Edward Island twist. Simple skewers of backyard chicken seared over the intense heat of our own homemade charcoal, then dipped in an apple cider–based tare sauce infused with deep mulled spice flavour before glazing and sprinkling with an Island-inspired blend of seven spices. A delicious homage to the intense heat of charcoal.

MAKE THE SEVEN-SPICE SPRINKLE

Preheat the oven to 350°F (180°C). Line a baking sheet with parchment paper.

Add the nori, pumpkin seeds, and chili flakes to a small food processor. Pulse into a coarse powder. Transfer to a small bowl, add the white and black sesame seeds and citrus zest, and mix well. Transfer the spice mixture to the lined baking sheet and spread into a thin, even layer. Turn off the oven and open the door to release the heat. Place the sheet in the oven. Close the door and let sit for an hour or so. Reserve or store in a small resealable container in a cool, dark place for up to 1 month.

MAKE THE MULLED CIDER TARE SAUCE

Preheat the oven to 425°F (220°C). Turn on the convection fan if you have one.

Pile the onions and garlic in the centre of a roasting pan. Cover with the chicken parts. Roast, uncovered, until the chicken is golden brown and caramelized, 30 minutes or so. Carefully pour off accumulated fat, reserving for another use. Transfer the chicken, onions, and garlic to a large saucepan. Pour the apple cider into the roasting pan and stir to dissolve all the browned bits. Pour into the saucepan. Add the soy sauce, brown sugar, cinnamon, bay leaves, peppercorns, allspice, and cloves. Bring to a slow, steady simmer, cover tightly, and cook until thickened and deeply infused with colour and flavour, 45 minutes. Remove the lid, increase the heat, and quickly reduce the sauce, thickening it to 2 cups (500 mL) or so. Remove from the heat and let sit until cool enough to handle. Pour through a fine-mesh strainer into a heatproof container. Refrigerate until cold and firm. Before using, remove any fat that congeals on the surface. The tare can be made 5 days before you need it.

PREP THE CHICKEN SKEWERS

Thread the meat onto the skewers, alternating chicken pieces with apples. Trim away any dangly chicken bits to prevent charring.

MAKES 12 SKEWERS, SERVES 4 TO 6

SPECIAL EQUIPMENT NEEDED: konro, hibachi, or ceramic kamado-style grill; binchotan charcoal or lump charcoal; 12 bamboo skewers, soaked in water overnight, or metal skewers; deep narrow tare pot (optional)

SEVEN-SPICE SPRINKLE (MAKES ABOUT 1 CUP/250 ML)

1 standard 8-inch (20 cm) square sheet nori, broken into small pieces
2 tablespoons (30 mL) pumpkin seeds
1 tablespoon (15 mL) red chili flakes
1 tablespoon (15 mL) white sesame seeds
1 tablespoon (15 mL) black sesame seeds
Zest of 1 orange
Zest of 1 lemon
Zest of 1 lime

MULLED CIDER TARE SAUCE (MAKES ABOUT 2 CUPS/500 ML)

2 large yellow or white cooking onions, peeled, quartered, broken into layers
Cloves from 1 head of garlic, peeled
1 pound (450 g) skin-on, bone-in chicken parts (necks, backs, carcass bones, or wings)
4 cups (1 L) fresh apple cider
2 cups (500 mL) soy sauce
1 cup (250 mL) firmly packed brown sugar
4 cinnamon sticks
4 bay leaves
1 tablespoon (15 mL) black peppercorns
1 tablespoon (15 mL) whole allspice
1 teaspoon (5 mL) whole cloves

APPLE CHICKEN SKEWERS

1½ pounds (675 g) boneless chicken (thigh or breast meat, with or without the skin, wings with wingtips removed, or livers), cut into 1½-inch (4 cm) pieces
2 large tart apples, unpeeled, cored, cut into 1-inch (2.5 cm) cubes

Recipe continues

BUILD A FIRE

Fill a fire basket with binchotan charcoal and ignite within the roaring flames of an active fire or within a charcoal chimney. Build a tightly packed single-layer charcoal fire in a konro or other charcoal grill. Alternatively, build a lump charcoal fire in a hibachi, kamado, or backyard charcoal grill. Cover carefully with a second layer of coals. Vigorously fan the coals to help fully ignite the charcoal. Tend to a growing bed of fiercely hot glowing white coals. The charcoal will progress through three distinct phases, from cold and black through surface ignition (indicated by an even feathery grey coat), before full ignition eventually penetrates to the centre and it begins glowing cherry red from within. If necessary, position skewer supports over the coals.

GRILL THE CHICKEN SKEWERS

Transfer the mulled cider tare sauce to a traditional tare pot or small saucepan and bring to a bare simmer to one side of the fire. Vigorously fan the coals to increase their searing heat. Place the chicken skewers directly on the konro edges or skewer supports. Cook the chicken like a human-powered rotisserie, turning and tending constantly, searing the meat until golden brown, tender, juicy, and nearly fully cooked, 5 minutes or so.

Remove the skewers from the heat, dip into the mulled cider tare sauce, return to the heat, and glaze, turning and tending constantly, a minute or so more. Dip and grill once or twice more, carefully glazing the chicken without scorching or burning. Remove from the heat, dip once more in the tare sauce, sprinkle with seven-spice, and serve immediately.

Briefly return any leftover tare sauce to a simmer, tightly cover, and refrigerate for regular use and replenishment or freeze in an airtight container for up to 6 months to begin your next batch.

SPICY VEGETABLE TACOS WITH HANDMADE TORTILLAS, GREEN LENTIL SMEAR, GRILLED OYSTER MUSHROOMS, VEGETABLE SLAW, AND CARROT JALAPEÑO HOT SAUCE

MAKES 50 (3-INCH/8 CM) OR 12 (8-INCH/20 CM) TORTILLAS, SERVES 12

Every day our raucous taco bar anchors one end of the Fire Garden during Oyster Hour. The toppings come and go but the basics of a classic taco endure. Handmade tortillas, lovingly toasted, smeared with a legume purée, piled high with snappy vegetable-forward toppings, and dressed with one of our many homemade hot sauces. Whether you try this version or create one of your own, you can rely on fire to help you toast and grill your way to authentic flavour.

SPECIAL EQUIPMENT NEEDED: large cast-iron plancha, griddle, or skillet

CARROT JALAPEÑO HOT SAUCE

2 cups (500 mL) peeled and grated carrots

1 yellow onion, grated

4 garlic cloves, minced

1 jalapeño pepper, halved, stem, seeds, and pith discarded, minced

½ cup (125 mL) orange juice

½ cup (125 mL) white wine vinegar or apple cider vinegar

1 teaspoon (5 mL) sea salt

2 tablespoons (30 mL) olive oil

1 tablespoon (15 mL) yellow mustard

GREEN LENTIL SMEAR

2 tablespoons (30 mL) butter or vegetable oil

1 tablespoon (15 mL) cumin seeds

1 large yellow onion, minced

4 garlic cloves, minced

1 cup (250 mL) green lentils

3 cups (750 mL) water

1 bay leaf

1 teaspoon (5 mL) salt

MAKE THE CARROT JALAPEÑO HOT SAUCE

Combine the carrots, onion, garlic, jalapeño, orange juice, white wine vinegar, and salt in a medium saucepan over medium-high heat. Bring to a slow, steady simmer for 5 minutes. Remove from the heat and let rest for 5 minutes more. Add the olive oil and mustard. Carefully blend until smooth with an immersion blender or in a high-speed blender. Transfer to a squeeze bottle and store in the refrigerator for up to 1 month.

MAKE THE GREEN LENTIL SMEAR

Toss the butter into a medium saucepan over medium-high heat. Swirl gently as it melts, steams, foams, and eventually lightly browns. Reduce the heat to low and stir in the cumin seeds. Continue stirring as their flavours emerge and brighten and the seeds lightly toast, about 1 minute. Stir in the onion and garlic. Cover tightly and cook, stirring occasionally, until the vegetables are soft and fragrant, 2 or 3 minutes more. Stir in the lentils, water, bay leaf, and salt. Bring to a slow, steady simmer, cover tightly, and cook for 20 minutes. Without uncovering, remove from the heat and let sit for another 10 minutes.

Discard the bay leaf. In a food processor, purée the lentil mixture until smooth. Serve warm or at room temperature. Store in a covered container in the refrigerator for up to 3 days.

Recipe and ingredients continue

MAKE THE TORTILLAS

In a large bowl, whisk together the flour, cornmeal, chili powder, and salt. Add the lard, crumbling and mixing with your fingers until thoroughly combined. Stir in the water until absorbed. On a lightly floured work surface, knead the dough until smooth. Wrap the dough in plastic wrap. Let rest and relax at room temperature for at least 20 minutes or refrigerate overnight.

Lightly flour a work surface, your hands, a rolling pin, and the dough. For 3-inch (8 cm) tortillas, pinch off a generous tablespoonful of dough and roll between your palms into a small, tight ball. For 8-inch (20 cm) tortillas, divide the dough into 12 pieces. For either size, roll the dough into a thin, even, round tortilla. Repeat with the remaining dough, stacking the tortillas between sheets of parchment paper. Refrigerate until firm, an hour or more.

MAKE THE VEGETABLE SLAW

In a medium bowl, whisk together the olive oil, cider vinegar, honey, mustard, salt, and hot sauce. Add the grated cabbage, carrots, and turnip and toss evenly. Cover and refrigerate until needed, up to 1 day.

BUILD A FIRE

Build and tend an active fire in your firepit, with a growing bed of glowing hot coals to one side. Position a grill grate over the fire and a large cast-iron plancha, griddle, or skillet over the coals, next to the active fire. Alternatively, light your charcoal grill or fire up your gas grill to its highest setting.

TOAST THE TORTILLAS

Judge the temperature of the preheated plancha to get a sense of timing. Cook the tortillas in batches without overcrowding the cooking surface and adjust the temperature as needed. Place tortillas on the hot surface and briefly sear the bottom, sealing the surface, for 15 seconds. Using a small spatula, flip over the tortillas and cook until the second side is lightly blistered and browned, even blackened a bit, about 1 minute. Flip the tortillas again and toast the first side until lightly browned. Serve immediately or let rest at room temperature. The cooled tortillas can be stored in a resealable container at room temperature for up to 2 days.

GRILL THE MUSHROOMS

Lightly season the mushrooms with salt and pepper, then position them on the hot grill. Sear, turning once, until tender and lightly browned, even crispy, 3 or 4 minutes total. Remove from the heat.

ASSEMBLE THE TACOS

Spread a spoonful of green lentil smear on each toasted tortilla. Top with a few mushrooms, a tangle of vegetable slaw, and a squirt of carrot jalapeño hot sauce.

HANDMADE TORTILLAS

2 cups (500 mL) all-purpose flour

1 cup (250 mL) fine cornmeal or whole wheat flour

1 tablespoon (15 mL) chili powder or ground or whole cumin or caraway seeds

½ teaspoon (2 mL) fine sea salt

8 tablespoons (125 mL) pure lard or butter, at room temperature

1 cup (250 mL) water

VEGETABLE SLAW

¼ cup (60 mL) olive oil

2 tablespoons (30 mL) apple cider vinegar

1 tablespoon (15 mL) pure liquid honey

1 tablespoon (15 mL) yellow mustard

1 teaspoon (5 mL) sea salt

½ teaspoon (2 mL) hot sauce

1 cup (250 mL) grated red cabbage

1 cup (250 mL) peeled and grated carrots

1 cup (250 mL) peeled and grated turnip

GRILLED OYSTER MUSHROOMS

1 pound (450 g) oyster mushrooms or any cultivated or foraged mushroom, washed and gently dried with paper towel

Sea salt

Freshly ground black pepper

TORTILLA TOASTING
Plancha Cooking Method

The handmade tortillas of authentic Mexican cooking are brought to life by properly toasting the dough. A quick sear on one side locks in steamy moisture before a longer flavourful browning of the second side and a return to the first side for finishing toasting.

ROTISSERIE CHICKEN WITH BAY SPICE RUB

A slowly rotating, generously spice-rubbed, juicy chicken, patiently rotisserie-roasted until golden brown and meltingly delicious. The epitome of elegant simplicity that's just as fun to roast as it is to eat.

BUILD A FIRE

For steady reflected heat, construct a small fireproof wall behind your firepit. Build and tend an active fire, with a growing bed of glowing hot coals. Position a rotisserie rig beside the fire, offset from the flames and direct heat (see page 46).

PREP THE CHICKEN

Place the chicken on a work surface. Using your hands, rub the chicken with olive oil, getting it in every nook and cranny until evenly coated. Wash and dry your hands. Generously season the chicken with bay spice. Skewer the lemon on the rotisserie spit, positioning it where the chicken will be. Run the spit and lemon through the chicken, pushing the lemon into the cavity and the rod out through the neck. The lemon will help steady the chicken from within. Secure both ends of the chicken with rotisserie forks. Adjust counterweight as needed.

ROAST THE CHICKEN

Position the spit on the rotisserie rig. Tend the fire to maintain steady medium heat. Roast the chicken, slowly turning and allowing the chicken to self-baste, until browned, tender, and juicy, 2 hours or so. The chicken is done when an instant-read probe thermometer in the thickest part of the breast meat and thigh registers at least 165°F (74°C). Let the fire die down but continue roasting as long as possible without overcooking the meat—if the thermometer hits 190°F (88°C), the meat will be dried out. Carefully remove the spit from the rig and the chicken from the spit. Transfer the chicken to a resting platter, cover loosely with foil, and let rest for 20 minutes before slicing. Carve or pull the chicken. Serve with an array of sides and salads.

SERVES 4 TO 6

SPECIAL EQUIPMENT NEEDED:
rotisserie rig; fireproof masonry or metal reflective wall behind and above the fire; digital instant-read probe thermometer

ROTISSERIE CHICKEN

1 large roasting chicken (about 4 pounds/1.8 kg), trussed
2 tablespoons (30 mL) olive oil
¼ cup (60 mL) Bay Spice (page 256)
1 lemon

ROTISSERIE ROASTING
Ancient Fire Kitchen Method

A mechanical means of rotating large cuts of meat as they roast to help them cook evenly. Constant slow rotation of the meat self-bastes the surface with its own juices, producing a characteristically mouth-watering appearance and flavour.

PORK BELLY TWIZZLERS WITH
MAPLE MUSTARD GLAZE

The incomparably exquisite flavour of uncured pork belly—fresh bacon—intensely seared, browned yet tender, meltingly juicy, smoked at the last second as its own juices drip over intensely hot charcoal and burst into flames.

MAKE THE MAPLE MUSTARD GLAZE

In a small bowl, whisk together the maple syrup, vegetable oil, and mustard. Reserve.

PREP THE PORK BELLY SKEWERS

Freeze the pork belly slab until firm but not frozen, 20 minutes or so. Using an electric deli slicer, thinly slice the pork, across the grain, into "half" bacon slices.

Starting at the top of each skewer, spiral each slice of pork around itself, with the meat to the inside and the fat on the outside. Cover tightly and refrigerate until needed.

BUILD A FIRE

Build a charcoal fire in a konro, hibachi, kamado, or backyard charcoal grill. Tend to a glowing bed of fiercely hot coals. If necessary, position supportive crossbars directly over the hottest coals.

GRILL THE PORK BELLY SKEWERS

Place the pork skewers on the grill edges or supports directly over the coals. Vigorously fan the coals to increase their searing heat. Cook the pork belly a minute or so, turning frequently, just until the surface sears. Remove the skewers from the heat and thoroughly brush with the maple mustard glaze. Return the skewers to the heat and continue searing another minute more, rotating continuously, setting the glaze until bubbling and lightly charred. Remove from the heat and brush once more with maple mustard glaze. Serve immediately.

SERVES 4 TO 6

SPECIAL EQUIPMENT NEEDED: konro, hibachi, kamado, or backyard charcoal grill; 12 bamboo skewers, soaked in water overnight, or metal skewers; pastry brush

MAPLE MUSTARD GLAZE
2 tablespoons (30 mL) pure maple syrup
1 tablespoon (15 mL) vegetable oil
1 tablespoon (15 mL) yellow mustard

1 skinless pork belly (1½ pounds/675 g), about 6 x 3 inches (15 x 8 cm)

CHARCOAL SEARING
Charcoal Cooking Method

Using the intense heat of live charcoal to flavourfully sear the surface of an ingredient so quickly that the heat doesn't have time to penetrate to the centre and overcook the interior. A live bed of glowing charcoal is among the very hottest heat options in the fire kitchen.

ÉCLADE DE MOULES (PINE NEEDLE–SMOKED MUSSELS) WITH LEMON THYME BROWN BUTTER

Along the coast of France where pine forests meet the Atlantic Ocean's edge, fisherfolk long ago discovered they could bury their catch under the plentiful dry needles and use their fragrant heat to cook a delicious meal. Their tradition came to Canada's shores with our Acadian community. Surprisingly the needle ash that covers the mussel shells tastes neither gritty nor burnt, instead infusing the mussel meat with delectable smokiness.

MAKE THE LEMON THYME BROWN BUTTER

Toss the butter into a small saucepan over medium-high heat. Swirl gently as it melts, steams, foams, and eventually lightly browns. Remove from the heat and immediately swirl in the fresh herb. Add the lemon zest and juice and lots of pepper. Reserve at room temperature until needed. Do not refrigerate.

PREP THE MUSSELS

In the centre of a 2-foot (60 cm) square board, form a shell support by driving 4 standard nails into the corners of a ¾-inch (2 cm) square. Use the nails as starting props to carefully begin stacking the mussels against each other in a self-supporting radial pattern. Pack them in as tightly as possible, orienting the mussels so they rest on their longest edge with their narrowest point towards the centre and their blunt hinge end toward the outside. (The hinged edges face up to prevent the shells from filling with ash.) Be patient—the spectacular result is worth the effort. Fifty or so mussels are the ideal mass for a single batch; any more and the middle mussels tend to undercook.

BUILD A FIRE

Layer the dry pine needles directly over the mussels, fluffing them with your fingers so they don't mat too densely, forming a 6-inch (15 cm) thick doughnut-like disc that extends over the edge of the pile. Leave a narrow chimney open in the centre to feed the fire and prevent matting. Ignite the edge in several places. Fan the flames with a cedar shingle or clipboard to help them spread evenly. Eventually the fire will go out, at which point vigorously fan away the ash. If the mussels have not fully opened, add another round of pine needles and ignite. The mussels are done when their shells steam open and cook the tender morsels within. Discard any mussels that did not open.

When the shells cool down, invite your guests to enjoy a feast by pulling the fragrant meat from a shell, then using the hinged shells as pincers to dip the tender smoky morsel into the fragrant lemon herb butter.

SERVES 6 TO 8 AS AN HORS D'OEUVRE, EASILY DOUBLED

SPECIAL EQUIPMENT NEEDED:

2-foot (60 cm) square board for shells; 4 standard nails; a bushel basketful of very dry pine needles, twigs and leaves sifted and discarded

LEMON THYME BROWN BUTTER

½ cup (125 mL) salted butter

A sprig or 2 of fresh thyme, rosemary, or sage

Zest and juice of 1 lemon

Freshly ground black pepper

50 or so live mussels (about 2.5 pounds/ 1.125 kg), rinsed well and beards removed

PINE NEEDLE SMOKING

Classic Fire Kitchen Method

Pine needles are a plentiful fuel but burn intensely hot and very quickly, thus limiting their practical use to rapid cooking techniques. They produce a sweet fragrant smoke and quickly vaporize into thin white ash.

WOOD OVEN–ROASTED VEGETABLES
WITH BONE MARROW DRESSING

The primal umami-rich flavours of luscious bone marrow extravagantly tossed with bright fresh herbs and simple homemade mustard to make an improvised dressing for fragrant wood oven–roasted vegetables. A truly decadent vegetable-forward treat and a reminder that meat is often at its best when it serves as a condiment for vegetables.

BUILD A FIRE
Build and tend an active fire in your wood oven, with live fire and glowing hot coals to the back and a clear roasting area to the front. Monitor the cooking temperature with an infrared thermometer. Tend the fire, bringing the oven to 500°F (260°C) or more. Preheat a large cast-iron skillet in the oven. Alternatively, fire up your indoor oven to its highest setting and turn on the convection fan if you have one.

ROAST THE BONE MARROW AND START THE DRESSING
In a very large cast-iron skillet (or 2 skillets if needed), arrange the marrow bones cut side up in a single layer. Season generously with salt and pepper. Roast in the wood-fired oven until the marrow fat is browned and bubbling around the edges. Remove from the oven. Handling carefully, scrape every drop of the rendered bone marrow into a medium bowl. Add the mustard and whisk until smooth. Reserve. Transfer the empty marrow bones to a serving platter.

MEANWHILE, ROAST THE VEGETABLES AND FINISH
Toss together the vegetable of your choice with the fat of your choice. Season with salt and pepper. Carefully transfer the vegetables to the preheated cast-iron skillet. Return to the oven and roast, searing, occasionally shaking and settling, until browned and lightly charred, 5 to 15 minutes depending on your vegetable. Transfer the vegetables to the bowl with the marrow dressing.

Add the parsley, tarragon, and chives to the bowl. Lightly toss together the roasted vegetables and bone marrow dressing. Spoon and mound the vegetable and marrow mixture back into the marrow bones. Garnish with the fresh herb sprigs.

SERVES 4 TO 8

SPECIAL EQUIPMENT NEEDED:
wood oven; high-temperature infrared thermometer; cast-iron skillets (1 or 2 large and 1 very large)

ROASTED BONE MARROW
4 beef shin bones (7 to 8 pounds/ 3.2 to 3.5 kg total), split lengthwise and trimmed into 6- to 8-inch (15 to 20 cm) lengths
Kosher salt
Freshly ground black pepper

BONE MARROW DRESSING
2 tablespoons (30 mL) grainy mustard
Leaves and tender stems from a handful of fresh curly or flat-leaf parsley sprigs, finely minced, a few small sprigs reserved for garnish
Leaves and tender stems from a handful of fresh tarragon sprigs, finely minced, a few small sprigs reserved for garnish
A handful of fresh chives, thinly sliced, a few whole chives reserved for garnish

WOOD OVEN–ROASTED VEGETABLES
2 to 3 pounds (900 g to 1.35 kg) of your favourite fresh vegetables suitable for roasting (potatoes, sweet potatoes, celery root, carrots, parsnips, turnips, sunchokes, onions; brassicas such as broccoli, cauliflower, brussels sprouts, kale; summer squash, zucchini, eggplant, tomatoes), prepped and cut into bite-size pieces
2 tablespoons (30 mL) bone marrow fat, other animal fat (beef, pork, duck, or chicken), or grapeseed oil
Kosher salt
Freshly ground black pepper

WOOD OVEN ROASTING
High-Heat Cooking Method

Harnessing the full heat potential of a wood oven to roast at sustained high temperatures in the presence of an active fire. Exquisitely browning an ingredient while imparting a wood roast flavour beyond that of slow smoke.

STICK BREAD WITH THREE BUTTER DIPS

Every scout's first campfire cooking trick elevated with a simple dough and your choice of a sweet buttery dip. Stick bread is as much an adventure as it is a treat, a way to connect to centuries of hunters camped out for the night, swapping flavours and stories around a campfire.

MAKE THE BREAD DOUGH

In a medium bowl, whisk together the all-purpose flour, whole wheat flour, yeast, sugar, and salt. Pour in the warm water and olive oil, switch to a wooden spoon, and stir together until a smooth dough forms. Cover the bowl with a kitchen towel and let rest in a warm place until the dough doubles in size, 1 hour or so.

BUILD A FIRE

Build and tend a slow fire in your firepit, bringing to medium heat with a glowing bed of hot coals.

PREPARE THE BREAD STICKS

Lightly flour your hands and work surface. Transfer the dough to the work surface and punch it down with your hands to release the air. Divide the dough into 8 equal pieces. One at a time, stretch and roll each portion of dough into a long sausage shape. Starting about an inch (2.5 cm) from the end, twist the dough around the stick, pressing the starting end of the dough into itself to secure, continuing in a spiral, and securely pinching the finishing end to itself.

BAKE THE BREAD

Prop the bread sticks next to the fire, positioning them over the coal bed but away from direct flames. Bake, turning frequently, until golden brown, tender, and fully cooked, 15 to 20 minutes.

MEANWHILE, MAKE THE BUTTER(S)

In a small pot near the fire, melt together the ingredients for your choice of butter. (Use separate pots if you are making more than one type of butter.) Enjoy the freshly baked bread by tearing it into strips and dipping into the melted butter.

SERVES 4 TO 8

SPECIAL EQUIPMENT NEEDED: 8 sticks (each 18 to 24 inches/46 to 60 cm long) from fresh green wood

STICK BREAD DOUGH

2 cups (500 mL) all-purpose flour

1 cup (250 mL) whole wheat flour

1 heaping teaspoon (7 mL) active dry yeast

1 teaspoon (5 mL) sugar

1 teaspoon (5 mL) sea salt

1 cup (250 mL) warm water

2 tablespoons (30 mL) olive oil

HONEY THYME BUTTER

8 tablespoons (125 mL) butter

2 tablespoons (30 mL) pure liquid honey

1 teaspoon (5 mL) finely minced fresh thyme

BROWN SUGAR CINNAMON BUTTER

8 tablespoons (125 mL) butter

2 tablespoons (30 mL) brown sugar

1 teaspoon (5 mL) cinnamon

ORANGE GINGER BUTTER

8 tablespoons (125 mL) butter

2 tablespoons (30 mL) orange marmalade

1 teaspoon (5 mL) finely grated frozen ginger

STICK BAKING
Fire Cooking Method

An ancient technique of wrapping dough around a stick, then placing near a fire to bake into bread. The dough is positioned in a lower heat zone that approximates that of a bread oven.

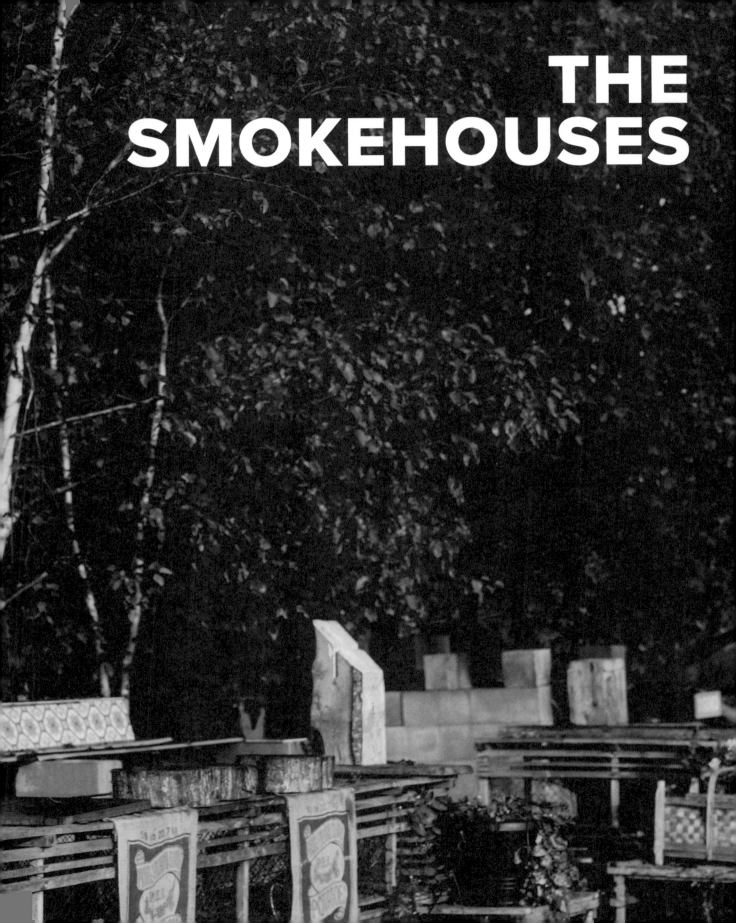

THE
SMOKEHOUSES

BEAST BRISKET WITH SALT, PEPPER, AND SMOKE

If grilling a burger is like showing up for the first day of kindergarten, then smoking a brisket is like earning your PhD. This deliciously beefy cut from the cow's breast is riddled with tough connective tissues that need long, patient softening without drying out the meat. Our Beast was built for the task, so meat can slowly absorb the essential heat and primal flavour of the gentle smoke and transform. With care its collagen will absorb ten times its own weight in moisture. Cooking this cut in a classic offset barrel smoker demands a certain Zen-like connection between the cook, the beef, the smoke, and the smokehouse. The effect is nothing short of magic.

BUILD A SMOKEHOUSE FIRE

Build and tend a slow, smouldering fire in the firebox of your offset smokehouse. Use your favourite smoking wood (see page 4) to create a slow, steady stream of aromatic smoke. Position a full water pan between the heat source and the eventual meat to help maintain moisture and consistent heat. Find the sweet spot where the smoky heat stabilizes between 225° and 250°F (110° to 120°C).

SEASON THE BRISKET

Place the brisket on a large baking sheet. Generously season the entire brisket with salt, favouring the thicker end (the point) with more salt than the thinner end (the flat). Repeat with pepper.

SMOKE THE BRISKET

Position the brisket in your smokehouse's sweet spot. Patiently smoke the brisket until its internal temperature reaches 203°F (95°C), 8 to 12 hours. Monitor the temperature with a remote sensor. The temperature will slowly climb to 150°F (65°C) or so before stalling for hours and hours, but eventually it will continue climbing again. By 203°F (95°C), the meat's connective tissue has magically softened, leaving the brisket tender and succulent. Remove from the smokehouse.

Wrap the brisket tightly in foil or butcher's paper and let rest in a tightly sealed picnic cooler for texture-improving carryover cooking, 2 to 3 hours more. During this essential time, moisture permeates the meat as it slowly cools to 160°F (70°C) and its texture relaxes.

Carefully unwrap the meat. Slice thinly across the grain with a serrated knife. Serve with an array of sides and salads.

SERVES 12

SPECIAL EQUIPMENT NEEDED: offset smokehouse; digital instant-read probe thermometer with a remote sensor; picnic cooler

1 beef brisket (12 pounds/5.4 kg), fatty side trimmed to ¼ inch (5 mm)
¼ cup (60 mL) sea salt
¼ cup (60 mL) freshly ground black pepper

SALT AND PEPPER
Pantry Staple

Common seasoning blend with hidden complexity and an essential secret for memorable smoking. Casually sprinkled salt seasons easily, but with care salt also unlocks texture and deeper favour. Pepper's bright, obvious heat can survive scorching flame, but its complex aromatic spice notes are revealed only through patient cooking.

SMOKED BEEFY RIBS WITH OLD-SCHOOL DRY RUB

Beef plate short ribs are big, meaty, and tender. These one-bone showstoppers are packed with intense beefy flavour, but to truly enjoy them, their strong, chewy texture must be patiently tamed until meltingly tender. A spicy salt rub and an overnight rest season the tough connective tissues before transformative patient smoking.

PREP THE RIBS

Generously rub the beef ribs on all sides with the old-school dry rub. Place the ribs in a baking pan or on a baking sheet, cover tightly with plastic wrap, and refrigerate overnight.

BUILD A SMOKEHOUSE FIRE

Build and tend a slow, smouldering fire in the firebox of your offset smokehouse. Use your favourite smoking wood (see page 4) to create a slow, steady stream of aromatic smoke. Position a full water pan between the heat source and the eventual meat to help maintain moisture and consistent heat. Find the sweet spot where the smoky heat stabilizes between 225° and 250°F (110° to 120°C).

SMOKE THE RIBS

Just before smoking, discard any accumulated juices. Position the ribs in your smokehouse's sweet spot. Patiently smoke the ribs until their internal temperature reaches 203°F (95°C), 6 to 8 hours. Monitor the temperature with a remote sensor as it slowly climbs. By 203°F (95°C), the meat's connective tissue has magically softened, leaving the meat tender and succulent. Remove from the smokehouse. Serve the ribs with an array of sides and salads.

SERVES 4

SPECIAL EQUIPMENT NEEDED: offset smokehouse; digital instant-read probe thermometer with a remote sensor

---

A 4-bone beef plate short rib roast (4 pounds/1.8 kg or so), cut into 4 ribs between the bones

½ cup (125 mL) Old-School Dry Rub (page 256)

DRY RUB
Pantry Staple

A mixture of salt, sugar, and signature, sometimes secret, aromatic spices unique to the cook or cuisine. A seasoning often applied in advance to allow time for the salt to penetrate the meat. An aromatic blend that helps develop the flavourful bark, or crust, of slowly cooked meat.

SPICY BEEFY JERKY

Long ago a practical cook in a smoky cave discovered the tasty potential of smoky dried meat, an easy way to transport lightweight nutrition and thus strength. Today we continue that tradition with local beef and flavours from our own global pantry. Our homemade jerky is pleasantly spicy, wonderfully chewy, and deeply beefy.

CURE THE JERKY

In a large metal bowl, whisk together the soy sauce, brown sugar, gochujang, and ginger. Stir in the meat ribbons, thoroughly coating with the marinade. Transfer to an extra-large resealable plastic bag, squeeze out the air, and tightly seal. Lay flat on a tray and refrigerate overnight.

BUILD A FIRE

Build and tend a slow, smouldering fire in the firebox of your offset smokehouse. Use your favourite smoking wood (see page 4) to create a slow, steady stream of aromatic smoke. Find the sweet spot where the smoky heat stabilizes between 150° and 160°F (65° to 70°C).

SMOKE THE JERKY

Place the jerky on mesh racks and position in the smokehouse. Smoke for 6 to 8 hours or longer, tending the fire, the smoke slowly smouldering and the heat low. Check on the progress every 30 minutes or so, adding more wood as needed, slowly infusing the beef strips with flavour without drying them out.

DEHYDRATE THE JERKY

Set a dehydrator to 160°F (70°C). Line the dehydrator tray with a silicone baking mat or parchment paper. Arrange the beef strips on the lined tray. Do not overlap the strips. Dehydrate until dry, 12 hours. Store in resealable plastic bags in the refrigerator for up to 1 month.

MAKES 2 POUNDS (900 G) OF JERKY

SPECIAL EQUIPMENT NEEDED: offset smokehouse; digital instant-read thermometer with a remote sensor; food dehydrator

2 cups (500 mL) dark soy sauce

2 cups (500 mL) firmly packed brown sugar

1 cup (250 mL) gochujang

1 (4-inch/10 cm) piece frozen unpeeled ginger, grated into a powder with a microplane

1 lean outside, bottom, or eye of round beef steak (5 pounds/2.25 kg), fat trimmed, sliced with the grain into long strips ¼ inch (5 mm) thick and 1 inch (2.5 cm) wide

SMOKE PRESERVING
Smoking Method

The low heat of prolonged aromatic wood smoking dries out the flesh of meat while adding powerful antimicrobial components that dramatically extend the shelf life of traditionally dried meats.

SMOKED CRACKED RIBS WITH OLD-SCHOOL DRY RUB AND ANCHO OR CHIPOTLE BARBECUE SAUCE

Deliciously smoky ribs shouldn't fall off the bone. Ribs are best with just the right amount of addictively chewy texture, tender and juicy but not soft and mushy. Classic dry rub seasons the meat, then combines with patient smoke to create the classic lacquered bark crust and tender juicy meat that characterizes perfectly smoked ribs. Barbecue sauce is saved for dipping!

BUILD A SMOKEHOUSE FIRE

Build and tend a slow, smouldering fire in the firebox of your offset smokehouse. Use your favourite smoking wood (see page 4) to create a slow, steady stream of aromatic smoke. Position a full water pan between the heat source and the eventual meat to help maintain moisture and consistent heat. Find the sweet spot where the smoky heat stabilizes between 225° and 250°F (110° to 120°C).

SEASON AND SMOKE THE RIBS

Lightly rub the baby back ribs on all sides with the old-school dry rub.

Position the racks in your smokehouse's sweet spot, curved bone side down, meaty side up. Patiently smoke the ribs until they are barely tender yet still delightfully chewy, 3 hours or so. The ribs are done when they pass the classic crack test: With a pair of tongs, firmly grasp one end of a rack across the bones and from beneath. Gently lift until the full rack is suspended. The ribs are done when the bark cracks once or twice across the surface, revealing the white meat within. Remove from the smokehouse.

Serve with ancho barbecue sauce, chipotle barbecue sauce, or your favourite sauce for dipping and an array of sides and salads.

SERVES 4 TO 6

SPECIAL EQUIPMENT NEEDED: offset smokehouse; digital instant-read thermometer with a remote sensor

8 racks of baby back ribs (about 8 pounds/ 3.5 kg total)

1 cup (250 mL) Old-School Dry Rub (page 256)

1 cup (250 mL) or so of Ancho Barbecue Sauce (page 260), Chipotle Barbecue Sauce (page 261), or your favourite sauce, for dipping

THE CRACK
Secret Cooking Method

A hard-earned insider's tip that shows when baby back ribs have reached the point of textural perfection. After long, slow cooking, the meat's strength will eventually yield, and at the surface, here and there, the lacquered bark will begin to break, or crack. An important waypoint before the meat goes too far, softens, loses texture, and falls off the bone.

MAPLE BRINED AND SMOKED PORK BELLY WITH SMOKED APPLESAUCE

Decadently rich, impossibly tasty pork belly, patiently brined with aromatic maple sugar, then ever so slowly smoked into juicy, tender submission with local maple hardwood. Sharp applesauce intriguingly smoked and thickened into a memorable condiment for the world of fire.

CURE THE PORK BELLY

In a small bowl, whisk together the maple sugar, salt, and pepper. Turn the pork belly skin side up. With a sharp knife, score the skin in a diamond pattern at 1-inch (2.5 cm) intervals, slicing about ½ inch (1 cm) deep. Flip over and season with half the maple sugar mixture. Flip back over and repeat with the remaining mixture, bending the meat to expose and season the inside of the fat as you do. Place the meat skin side up in a large pan. Cover tightly with plastic wrap and refrigerate for 8 to 12 hours.

BUILD A SMOKEHOUSE FIRE

Build and tend a slow, smouldering fire in the firebox of your offset smokehouse. Use well-seasoned maple or your favourite hardwood (see page 4) to create a slow, steady stream of aromatic smoke. Position a full water pan between the heat source and the eventual meat to help maintain moisture and consistent heat. Find the sweet spot where the smoky heat stabilizes between 225° and 250°F (110° to 120°C).

SMOKE THE PORK BELLY

Discard accumulated juices. Position the pork belly in your smokehouse's sweet spot. Patiently smoke the meat until meltingly tender and juicy, 6 hours or so. Monitor the temperature with a remote sensor. It's ready when the internal temperature reaches 190°F (88°C). Remove from the smokehouse.

Wrap the pork belly tightly in foil or butcher's paper and let rest in a tightly sealed picnic cooler to slowly cool to 160°F (70°C), allowing the meat to reabsorb moisture and its texture to relax, 1 hour. (Once relaxed and cooled, the pork belly can be chilled until firm or refrigerated for up to 2 days, then cut into 4-inch/10 cm cubes. Pan-fry, roast, or deep-fry to reheat.)

MEANWHILE, MAKE THE SMOKED APPLESAUCE

In a cast-iron Dutch oven, combine the apples, brown sugar, cider vinegar, cinnamon, chili flakes, cumin, salt, and cloves. Stir together thoroughly. Cover tightly, place in the smokehouse with the pork belly, and gently cook until the apples are tender and release their juices, 2 hours or so. Remove from the smokehouse. Purée until smooth with an immersion blender, then return to the smokehouse, uncovered. (Alternatively, just remove the lid and skip the puréeing.) Continue smoking for another few hours, stirring thoroughly every 15 minutes, thickening and darkening the mixture. Transfer to a serving bowl.

Unwrap the pork belly and slice carefully with a serrated knife. Serve with spoonfuls of smoked applesauce and an array of sides and salads.

SERVES 12 OR MORE

SPECIAL EQUIPMENT NEEDED: offset smokehouse; cast-iron Dutch oven; digital instant-read probe thermometer with a remote sensor; picnic cooler

MAPLE PORK BELLY

½ cup (125 mL) maple sugar

¼ cup (60 mL) coarse sea salt or Diamond Crystal kosher salt

2 tablespoons (30 mL) freshly ground black pepper

1 skin-on pork belly (10 to 12 pounds/ 4.5 to 5.4 kg)

SMOKED APPLESAUCE

5 pounds (2.25 kg) Honeycrisp or other tart apples, unpeeled, cored, finely diced

2 cups (500 mL) firmly packed brown sugar

1 cup (250 mL) apple cider vinegar

1 tablespoon (15 mL) cinnamon

1 teaspoon (5 mL) red chili flakes

1 teaspoon (5 mL) ground cumin

½ teaspoon (2 mL) salt

¼ teaspoon (1 mL) ground cloves

MAPLE SUGAR
Pantry Staple

The pure crystalline sugar produced by further evaporating and concentrating liquid maple syrup. Maple sugar has a deeper flavour than its precursor maple syrup and its dry texture means it is easily combined with salt and seasonings.

DOUBLE-SMOKED BACON

Bacon is crispy preserved smoke. Pork belly magnificently absorbs the addictive flavours of aromatic smoke, saving them for another day in the form of bacon. Slowly cured and smoked not once but twice so a thick slice can land in a sizzling pan.

MAKES 10 POUNDS (4.5 KG) OF SMOKED BACON

SPECIAL EQUIPMENT NEEDED:
large non-reactive container; offset smokehouse; digital instant-read probe thermometer with a remote sensor

BROWN SUGAR CURED BACON
4 quarts (4 L) cold water
220 g sea salt
200 g brown sugar
30 g pink curing salt #1 (see note below)
1 skinless pork belly (10 to 12 pounds/ 4.5 to 5.4 kg)

PEPPERCORN CRUST
100 g coarsely ground black pepper
25 g juniper berries
25 g whole allspice
25 g coriander seeds

PINK CURING SALT #1
Fire Kitchen Ingredient

A mixture of sodium chloride and sodium nitrate used as an essential curing agent in preserved meats to safely extend shelf life while maintaining colour and flavour. Commonly dyed pink so it doesn't get confused with similar-tasting table salt.

BRINE THE PORK BELLY
In a large non-reactive container that will fit the pork belly, stir together the cold water, sea salt, brown sugar, and pink curing salt until fully dissolved. Sink the pork belly into the brine and weigh it down with a small plate or two to keep it submerged. Cover tightly with a lid or plastic wrap and refrigerate for 5 days.

PEPPERCORN-CRUST THE BELLY
Combine the pepper, juniper berries, allspice, and coriander seeds in a spice grinder or dedicated coffee grinder. Grind into a coarse powder. Remove the bacon from the brine and drain. Sprinkle both sides evenly with the pepper-corn mixture.

BUILD A SMOKEHOUSE FIRE
Build and tend a slow, smouldering fire in the firebox of your offset smokehouse. Use your favourite smoking wood (see page 4) to create a slow, steady stream of aromatic smoke. Position a full water pan between the heat source and the eventual meat to help maintain moisture and consistent heat. Find the sweet spot where the smoky heat stabilizes between 100° and 150°F (38° to 65°C). In the last hour or so of smoking gradually stoke the fire, raising the heat enough to bring the bellies internal temperature up.

DOUBLE-SMOKE THE BACON
Hang the bacon in the smokehouse chamber or place it on a wire-mesh shelf. Patiently smoke the belly, slowly perfuming its surface with aromatic smoke. Monitor the meat's temperature with a remote sensor. When the internal temperature reaches 160°F (70°C), after 6 hours or so, remove the meat from the smokehouse. Let rest until cool, then tightly wrap in plastic wrap and refrigerate overnight.

The next day, rebuild the smokehouse fire and continue smoking the bacon, adding another layer of smoky flavour, continuing until the internal temperature reaches 160°F (70°C), 3 hours or so. Remove from the smokehouse and let rest until cool. Tightly wrap in plastic wrap and refrigerate overnight again as the bacon firms and its smoky flavours mellow.

Continue for a third or fourth day if you like, but as the bacon smokes never allow its internal temperature to exceed 160°F (70°C). Wrap in plastic wrap and store in the refrigerator for up to 1 week or in a vacuum-sealed bag for up to 1 month.

CRISP THE BACON
Cut the firm cold bacon into thick, even slices. Preheat a large non-stick or cast-iron skillet over medium-low heat. Arrange the bacon slices in a single layer. Slowly, patiently fry until rendered, sizzling, and lightly browned, 10 minutes or so. Flip over and continue until cooked to your liking.

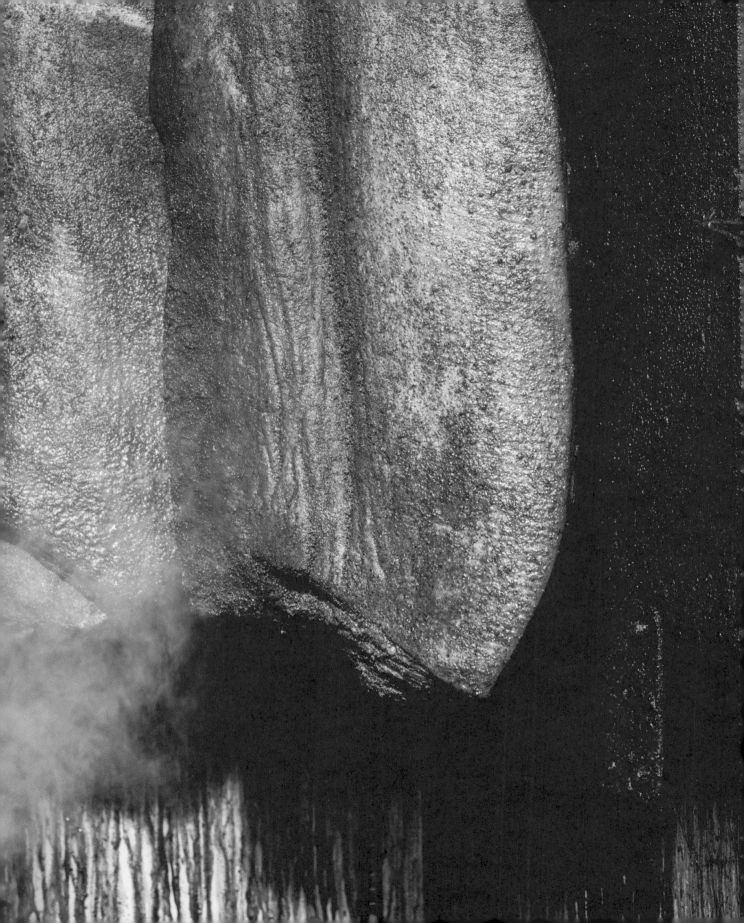

PULLED PORK SHOULDER BARBECUE SANDWICHES WITH OL' COLESLAW

Tender, meltingly juicy, hauntingly smoky pork shoulder, slowly transformed by the aromatic heat of our smokehouse. A simple spice rub and a patient rest for penetrating flavour. A moist mop for juicy basting. Soft roll sandwiches. Tangy coleslaw and your favourite spicy sauce.

SEASON THE PORK SHOULDER

Generously massage the meat all over with the old-school dry rub. Transfer the pork to a baking sheet, cover tightly with plastic wrap, and refrigerate for at least 2 hours or overnight.

BUILD A SMOKEHOUSE FIRE

Build and tend a slow, smouldering fire in the firebox of your offset smokehouse. Use your favourite smoking wood (see page 4) to create a slow, steady stream of aromatic smoke. Position a full water pan between the heat source and the eventual meat to help maintain moisture and consistent heat. Find the sweet spot where the smoky heat stabilizes between 225° and 250°F (110° to 120°C).

PREPARE THE MOP

In a small bowl, whisk together the cider vinegar, cider, Worcestershire sauce, vegetable oil, salt, and pepper. Have ready a food-safe basting mop.

SMOKE THE PORK SHOULDER

Discard any accumulated juices. Position the two pork shoulder halves in your smokehouse's sweet spot. Patiently smoke the shoulders until tender and juicy, turning and thoroughly brushing and basting with the mop every 45 minutes or so, 8 to 12 hours. Monitor the meat's internal temperature with a remote sensor. The temperature will slowly climb to 160°F (70°C) or so before stalling for hours and hours. Discontinue mopping, leaving the meat undisturbed. Eventually the temperature will continue climbing again. By 203°F (95°C), the connective tissues have magically softened. Remove from the smokehouse, transfer to a roasting pan, and let rest until cool enough to handle.

MAKE THE OL' COLESLAW

In a medium bowl, whisk together the mayonnaise, onion, dill pickle and juice, capers, horseradish, brown sugar, celery seeds, and salt until well combined.

Fit a food processor with the thin slicing blade and slice the cabbage into thin shreds. (Alternatively, use a sharp knife.) Add the shredded cabbage and the carrots to the dressing. Toss the works until evenly coated.

PULL THE PORK SHOULDER

When the smoked pork shoulder is cool, using tongs and large forks, shred into large bite-size pieces. Stir with the accumulated juices. Mound the pork onto the bottom of each bun, drizzle with ancho barbecue sauce, top with coleslaw, and close the sandwiches. Serve with lots of extra ancho barbecue sauce and an array of sides and salads.

SERVES 12

SPECIAL EQUIPMENT NEEDED: offset smokehouse; digital instant-read probe thermometer with a remote sensor; small food-safe basting mop

1 bone-in pork shoulder roast (Boston butt; about 5 pounds/2.25 kg), halved
½ cup (125 mL) Old-School Dry Rub (page 256)

THE MOP

1 cup (250 mL) apple cider vinegar
½ cup (125 mL) fresh apple cider, apple juice, or water
2 tablespoons (30 mL) Worcestershire sauce
1 tablespoon (15 mL) vegetable oil
1 tablespoon (15 mL) sea salt
1 tablespoon (15 mL) black pepper

OL' COLESLAW

½ cup (125 mL) mayonnaise
¼ cup (60 mL) minced yellow or white onion
¼ cup (60 mL) minced dill pickle
2 tablespoons (30 mL) dill pickle juice
¼ cup (60 mL) minced drained capers
2 tablespoons (30 mL) prepared horseradish
1 tablespoon (15 mL) brown sugar
1 teaspoon (5 mL) celery seeds
1 teaspoon (5 mL) sea salt
1 head of white or green cabbage, quartered, cores removed
1 large or 2 smaller carrots, peeled and grated

FOR THE BARBECUE SANDWICHES

12 soft burger buns, split
2 cups (500 mL) Ancho Barbecue Sauce (page 260), more for serving as needed

THE MOP
Traditional Barbecue Tool

A food-safe mop used to efficiently brush flavourful moisture onto the surface of slowly smoking meat, preventing it from drying out while improving texture and taste.

SMOKE-ROASTED CHICKEN WINGS
WITH ANCHO SPICE RUB AND BLUE CHEESE AIOLI

Succulent, not-too-spicy chicken wings, deeply flavoured with smoky spices and fragrant chilies, aromatically smoke-roasted, dipped into the rich, garlicky goodness of a classic aioli beefed up with umami-rich blue cheese.

MAKE THE ANCHO SPICE RUB AND SEASON THE CHICKEN WINGS
In a small bowl, whisk together the brown sugar, salt, ancho chili powder, chili powder, cumin, garlic powder, and cayenne pepper.

In a large bowl, generously season the wings with half the rub, tossing to coat evenly. Transfer the wings to a baking sheet, cover tightly with plastic wrap, and refrigerate for at least 2 hours or overnight. Transfer the remaining dry rub to a mason jar, tightly seal, and store in a cool, dark place for your next smoky project.

BUILD A SMOKEHOUSE FIRE
Build and tend a steady, hot fire in the firebox of your offset smokehouse. Use your favourite smoking wood (see page 4) to create a slow, steady stream of aromatic smoke. Position a full water pan between the heat source and the eventual meat to help maintain moisture and consistent heat. Find the sweet spot where the smoky heat stabilizes at about 325°F (160°C).

SMOKE-ROAST THE CHICKEN WINGS
Discard accumulated juices. Position the chicken wings in your smokehouse's sweet spot. Smoke-roast until brown and tender, an hour or so. The chicken is done when an instant-read thermometer in the thickest part of the meat registers 165°F (74°C). For a deeper smoky flavour, lower the smokehouse heat to 250°F (120°C) and continue smoking for another hour or so.

MEANWHILE, MAKE THE BLUE CHEESE AIOLI
Grate the garlic with a microplane into a paste. (Alternatively, mince the garlic, then mash under the side of a knife.) To a food processor, add the garlic, blue cheese, egg yolk, cider vinegar, salt, and cayenne pepper and process until smooth. With the machine running, add the grapeseed oil in a slow, steady stream until a thick emulsion forms. Transfer to a bowl for dipping.

Serve the smoked wings with lots of blue cheese aioli for dipping and an array of sides and salads.

SERVES 4 TO 6

SPECIAL EQUIPMENT NEEDED: offset smokehouse; digital instant-read thermometer

SMOKE-ROASTED CHICKEN WINGS
24 chicken wings (4 to 5 pounds/ 1.8 to 2.25 kg)

ANCHO SPICE RUB (MAKES ABOUT 2¼ CUPS/550 ML)
1 cup (250 mL) firmly packed brown sugar
¾ cup (175 mL) Diamond Crystal kosher salt
¼ cup (60 mL) ancho chili powder
¼ cup (60 mL) chili powder
2 tablespoons (30 mL) ground cumin
1 tablespoon (15 mL) garlic powder
1 teaspoon (5 mL) cayenne pepper

BLUE CHEESE AIOLI
2 large garlic cloves, peeled and halved
4 ounces (115 g) blue cheese, Roquefort, Stilton, Gorgonzola, or Cabrales, at room temperature
1 large organic egg yolk
1 tablespoon (15 mL) apple cider vinegar
¼ teaspoon (1 mL) sea salt
Pinch of cayenne pepper
½ cup (125 mL) grapeseed or olive oil

SMOKE ROASTING
Smoking Spectrum Method

To cook at traditional roasting temperatures while simultaneously smoking an ingredient. Smoking at the highest end of the heat spectrum. To roast in a smoke-filled chamber.

HOT-SMOKED SALMON WITH BAY SPICE CURE AND BLACK APPLE AIOLI

We smoke our legendary salmon every day in our Lighthouse Smokehouse and serve it during Oyster Hour in our Fire Garden at the inn. The fish is first cured for several days, seasoning and firming its flesh, before it spends a day in the smokehouse with one of our various fragrant local woods. Aromatic fermented, or black, apples anchor one of our favourite accompanying condiments.

CURE THE SALMON
Place the salmon skin side down in a baking dish or on a baking sheet. Sprinkle 1 cup (250 mL) of the bay spice evenly over the flesh and pat it with your fingers into a thick, even layer. Cover with plastic wrap laid directly over the fish and refrigerate overnight.

By the next day the fish will have extruded moisture and its texture will have firmed up. Turn the fillet over into the sugary brine. Cover and refrigerate another day or two.

Under cold running water, gently rinse off the cure but don't dry the fish. Rinse the pan and return the fish to it skin side down. Lightly sprinkle with the remaining 1 tablespoon (15 mL) bay spice. Refrigerate before smoking.

BUILD A SMOKEHOUSE FIRE
Build and tend a slow, smouldering fire in the firebox of your offset smokehouse. Use your favourite smoking wood (see page 4) to create a slow, steady stream of aromatic smoke. Position a full water pan between the heat source and the eventual salmon to help maintain moisture and consistent heat. Find the sweet spot where the smoky heat stabilizes around 150° to 160°F (65° to 70°C).

SMOKE THE SALMON
Position the moist salmon fillet in the smokehouse. Smoke for 4 to 6 hours, tending the fire, the smoke slowly smouldering and the heat low, checking on progress every 30 minutes or so, adding more wood as needed, slowly infusing the salmon with flavour without drying it out. Check the internal temperature of the salmon with an instant-read thermometer; it's done when it exceeds 165°F (74°C). If necessary, briefly stoke the fire to finish heating the fish. Serve warm from the smokehouse or let rest until cool. Store in the refrigerator, wrapped tightly in plastic wrap, for up to 5 days or freeze for up to 3 months.

MAKE THE AIOLI
In a food processor, purée the black apple with the cider vinegar until smooth. Add the egg yolk and, with the machine running, add the grapeseed oil in a slow, steady stream until a smooth emulsion forms. Season with salt and cayenne pepper. Transfer to a squeeze bottle.

Serve as an hors d'oeuvre, atop your favourite festive crackers, squirted with black apple aioli. Alternatively, cut into individual portions and enjoy topped with the aioli as an entrée with your favourite vegetables or salad.

SERVES 24 AS AN HORS D'OEUVRE OR 6 TO 8 AS A MAIN COURSE

SPECIAL EQUIPMENT NEEDED: offset smokehouse; digital instant-read probe thermometer with a remote sensor; digital instant-read thermometer

HOT-SMOKED SALMON
1 side of sustainably sourced skin-on salmon (about 4 pounds/1.8 kg; see page 263)
1 cup + 1 tablespoon (265 mL) Bay Spice (page 256), divided

BLACK APPLE AIOLI
1 black (fermented) apple (or cloves from 1 head of black garlic, peeled)
1 tablespoon (15 mL) apple cider vinegar
1 large organic egg yolk
½ cup (125 mL) grapeseed oil
½ teaspoon (2 mL) sea salt
Pinch of cayenne pepper

Crackers, for serving

HOT-SMOKING
Smokehouse Method

Slowly smoking fish or meat with just enough heat to eventually cook its flesh. Mastery lies in barely maintaining the slow smoky heat for many long hours without overcooking and drying out the food.

WINTER SMOKED SALMON WITH BAY SPICE CURE, HORSERADISH DILL BOURSIN, AND PICKLED RED ONIONS

Rich, luscious slices of cold-smoked salmon, firmly cured and perfumed with our signature blend of aromatics. Winter smoked for days with low temperatures for gentle flavour. Impeccably frozen until summer service with a traditionally bright condiment.

CURE THE SALMON
Place the salmon skin side down in a baking dish or on a baking sheet. Sprinkle 1 cup (250 mL) of the bay spice evenly over the flesh and pat with your fingers into a thick, even layer. Cover with plastic wrap laid directly over the fish and refrigerate overnight.

By the next day the fish will have extruded moisture and its texture will have firmed up. Turn the fillet over into the sugary brine. Cover and refrigerate another day or two.

Under cold running water, gently rinse off the cure but don't dry the fish. Rinse the pan and return the fish to it skin side down. Lightly sprinkle with the remaining 1 tablespoon (15 mL) bay spice. Refrigerate 1 full day before smoking.

BUILD A WINTER SMOKEHOUSE FIRE
When days of freezing weather are forecast, build and tend a slow, smouldering fire in the firebox of a winter smokehouse. Use your favourite smoking wood (see page 4) to create a steady stream of aromatic smoke. Find the sweet spot where the smoky heat stabilizes at or below 70°F (21°C). Above 86°F (30°C) the texture of the fish firms and begins to flake.

SMOKE THE SALMON
Position the firm salmon fillets in the smokehouse. Smoke, tending the fire, the smoke slowly smouldering and the heat low, checking on progress every hour or two, adding more wood as needed, slowly infusing the salmon with flavour. Smoke for at least 24 hours, or if the outside temperature remains low, 2 to 3 days for even more impressive results.

Wrap tightly in plastic wrap and refrigerate for at least 24 hours before serving. Store in the refrigerator for up to 5 days or seal in a vacuum bag to freeze for up to a year. Thaw slowly in the refrigerator for several days before serving.

MAKE THE HORSERADISH DILL BOURSIN
In a small bowl, with a wooden spoon, stir together the Boursin, horseradish, and dill. Reserve or transfer to a 1-cup (250 mL) mason jar or similar tightly sealed container and refrigerate for up to 5 days.

To serve, thinly slice the smoked salmon at a 45-degree angle. Serve as an hors d'oeuvre, atop bagels smeared with dollops of horseradish dill Boursin. Top with pickled red onions and garnish with fresh dill sprigs.

SERVES 24 AS AN HORS D'OEUVRES

SPECIAL EQUIPMENT NEEDED: offset smokehouse; digital instant-read thermometer with a remote sensor

WINTER-SMOKED SALMON WITH BAY SPICE CURE
1 side of sustainably sourced skin-on salmon (4 pounds/1.8 kg; see page 263)
1 cup (250 mL) + 1 tablespoon (15 mL) Bay Spice (page 256), divided

HORSERADISH DILL BOURSIN (MAKES ABOUT 1 CUP/250 ML)
1 small wheel (50 g) Garlic & Fine Herbs Boursin cheese (or ⅔ cup/150 mL plain cream cheese), at room temperature
2 tablespoons (30 mL) prepared horseradish
Leaves and tender stems from 1 bunch of fresh dill, minced, a few sprigs reserved for garnish

FOR SERVING
Your favourite bagels, artisanal bread toast, or crackers
½ cup (125 mL) Pickled Red Onions (page 257)

COLD-SMOKING
Smokehouse Method

Smoking at low temperature so that fish or meat is deeply flavoured but not cooked by heat. Preserving food by safely curing with salt, prolonged smoking, and dehydration. Traditionally a winter preservation method when outside ambient temperatures are reliably lower and safer.

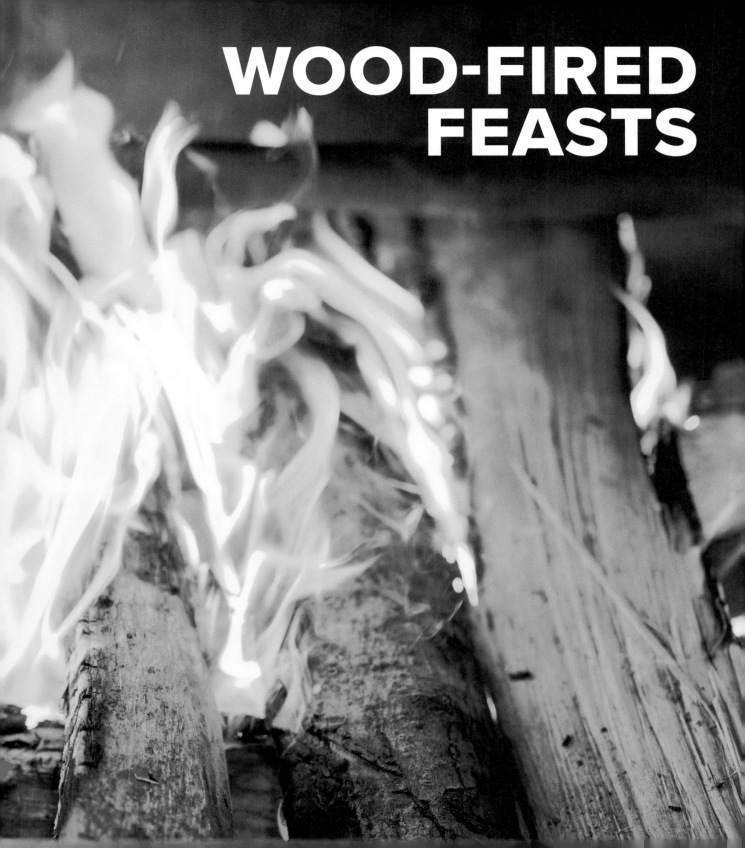

WOOD-FIRED FEASTS

WOOD-ROASTED FENNEL-STUFFED PORCHETTA (SANDWICHES) WITH SALSA VERDE

This is a spectacular way to feed a crowd with a showstopping centrepiece and one of the most mouth-watering sandwiches known to humans. Slowly roasted porchetta, the pride of Italians everywhere, perfumed with traditional fennel, layered on soft sourdough buns slathered with bright, tangy salsa verde.

MAKE THE SALSA VERDE

To a food processor, add the shallots, anchovies, capers, garlic, red wine vinegar, mustard, and salt. Pulse, scraping down the sides once or twice, until thoroughly combined into a thick paste. Add the parsley and olive oil and continue processing until smoothly puréed. Reserve in a small jar or bowl or store in a resealable container in the refrigerator for up to 1 month.

MARINATE THE PORK

In a small dry skillet over medium heat, warm the fennel and coriander seeds until fragrant and toasted, a minute or so. Transfer the toasted seeds with the bay leaves to a spice grinder or dedicated coffee grinder and grind into a coarse grainy powder. Transfer to a small bowl. Add the garlic, lemon zest and juice, mustard, olive oil, and chili flakes. Whisk together well.

Lay the pork belly skin side down on a work surface. Score the meaty surface in a diamond pattern at 1-inch (2.5 cm) intervals, slicing about ½ inch (1 cm) deep. Place the pork skin side up in a large baking pan. Cover all over with the marinade, rubbing it into the crevices. Cover tightly with plastic wrap and refrigerate for at least 12 hours or overnight.

PREP THE PORCHETTA

Cover the flesh side of the pork belly with the shaved fennel and chopped fennel fronds. Starting with a longer edge, roll the meat into a tight log shape. Position the roast seam side down and tightly tie with butcher's string at 2-inch (5 cm) intervals. Thread the rotisserie spit through the centre of the roast and secure on the ends with prongs. Sprinkle the entire surface evenly with the salt and baking powder.

BUILD A FIRE

For steady reflected heat, construct a small fireproof wall behind your firepit. Build and tend an active fire, with a growing bed of glowing hot coals. Position the rotisserie rig beside the fire, offset from the flames and direct heat (see page 46).

Recipe continues

SPECIAL EQUIPMENT NEEDED:
rotisserie rig; masonry or metal reflective wall behind fire; digital instant-read probe thermometer

SALSA VERDE
2 shallots, sliced
2 anchovy fillets
2 tablespoons (30 mL) drained capers
4 garlic cloves, sliced
2 tablespoons (30 mL) red wine vinegar
1 teaspoon (5 mL) grainy mustard
½ teaspoon (2 mL) salt
1 bunch of fresh flat-leaf parsley
1 cup (250 mL) extra-virgin olive oil

WOOD-ROASTED FENNEL-STUFFED PORCHETTA
¼ cup (60 mL) fennel seeds
¼ cup (60 mL) coriander seeds
12 bay leaves
Cloves from 1 head of garlic, finely minced
Zest and juice of 2 lemons
1 cup (250 mL) Dijon mustard
½ cup (125 mL) olive oil
2 tablespoons (30 mL) red chili flakes
1 pork belly, rind intact, rib meat attached (12 to 15 pounds/5.4 to 6.8 kg)
1 fennel bulb, trimmed, halved, cored, and thinly shaved crosswise on a mandoline, feathery fronds finely chopped
2 tablespoons (30 mL) salt
1 tablespoon (15 mL) baking powder

FOR THE SANDWICHES
12 to 16 soft sourdough or focaccia rolls
10 ounces (280 g) fresh arugula

ROAST THE PORCHETTA

Position the spit on the rotisserie rig. Tend the fire, maintaining steady heat and active flames, occasionally crisscrossing new fuel onto the embers. Roast, slowly turning and allowing the roast to self-baste, until browned, tender, and juicy, 3 hours or so. Once an instant-read thermometer in the thickest part of the meat registers 160°F (70°C), let the pork linger but allow the fire to die down and the meat to begin cooling.

Carefully remove the spit from the rig and the roast from the spit. Transfer to a resting platter, cover loosely with foil, and let rest for 20 minutes before slicing.

ASSEMBLE THE SANDWICHES

Split the rolls and spread with salsa verde. Stuff the sandwiches with thick slices of fragrant porchetta, topped with tangy arugula.

PORCHETTA
Fire Kitchen Method

A classic Italian preparation of pork belly rolled around its adjacent loin and slowly roasted to perfection over an open fire. The dish is known for its juicy, tender, fragrant meat contrasting with its crispy, crusty skin. There are many regional variations. Some avoid the peril of modern lean pork loins drying out by using shoulder cuts or just the belly.

ASADOR LAMB WITH MINT CHIMICHURRI

An entire lamb, rubbed with aromatic spices, slowly roasted on a large metal frame next to a slow, smoky campfire, basted with honey mustard, then served with one of Argentina's greatest gifts to the world of fire and flame: chimichurri. In Argentina, traditional asador is as much an occasion as it is a way of cooking, the cook themselves, and a specific piece of gear.

PREPARE THE LAMB AND BASTING SAUCE

Sprinkle the old-school dry rub evenly over the entire lamb, both sides and into all the nooks and crannies of the carcass. With strong wire, firmly attach the lamb to the metal frame.

In a medium bowl, whisk together the cider vinegar, mustard, and honey for basting. Reserve.

MAKE THE MINT CHIMICHURRI

To a food processor, add the garlic, red wine vinegar, olive oil, and water. Process until smooth. Add the chili flakes, cumin, salt, and mint. Process until the leaves are finely chopped and a smooth, fragrant paste emerges. Transfer to a side bowl or two, cover, and let rest until the flavours develop, at least 30 minutes or overnight. Leftovers can be stored in the refrigerator for up to 1 month.

BUILD A FIRE

For steady reflected heat, build and tend a small active campfire against the back of a large fireplace, smoke shed, or a small fireproof wall partially built around your firepit.

ROAST THE LAMB

Lean the lamb next to but not directly over the fire, offset from the direct heat of the scorching flames but well within the range of their smoky heat. When the meat begins to sizzle and sear, frequently and thoroughly baste, using the herb bouquet or a barbecue brush. Briefly lean the frame back from the fire to reach the meat facing the fire. Continue cooking and basting for hours, slowly tenderizing the meat's many muscles, rotating the works every hour or so to maintain even cooking. Monitor the meat's internal temperature with a digital probe thermometer. The lamb is done when it reaches 145°F (63°C), but truly delicious when it only stays there for a while. Plan on at least 4 hours, 6 if you can slow down the fire and hold the meat's temperature steady.

Remove the lamb from the frame and present with as much festive flair as you can to as many family and friends as you can find. Carve the meat thinly and serve with lots of mint chimichurri, a large green salad, and an array of vegetable sides.

SERVES 24

SPECIAL EQUIPMENT NEEDED: asador metal frame; stainless-steel wire; electrician's pliers; digital instant-read thermometer

ASADOR LAMB

1 whole lamb, ethically raised and butchered, head removed, gutted and split but not halved (about 45 pounds/ 20 kg)
1 batch Old-School Dry Rub (page 256)

BASTING SAUCE

4 cups (1 L) apple cider vinegar
2 cups (500 mL) Dijon or yellow mustard
1 cup (250 mL) pure liquid honey
A thick bouquet of fresh herbs with strong stems (sage, rosemary, thyme, lavender, fennel, and/or tarragon; optional)

MINT CHIMICHURRI

Cloves from 2 heads of garlic, peeled
1 cup (250 mL) red wine vinegar
1 cup (250 mL) extra-virgin olive oil
1 cup (250 mL) water
1 tablespoon (15 mL) red chili flakes
1 tablespoon (15 mL) ground cumin
1 teaspoon (5 mL) sea salt
Leaves and tender stems from 1 pound (450 g) of fresh mint

ASADOR FRAME
Fire Cooking Tool

A large metal frame designed to secure a splayed whole animal in the indirect heat of a fire, allowing for easy handling during prolonged cooking.

BRAISED AND CHARRED BEEF SHANK
TACOS WITH GRILLED CHILI SALSA

Deeply beefy and exquisitely charred tender beef shanks transformed by the fire and an intriguing technique for these legendary tacos.

BRAISE THE BEEF SHANK

Preheat the oven to 325°F (160°C). Turn on the convection fan if you have one. Fill a large Dutch oven with the onions, garlic, guajillo and ancho chilies, bay leaves, fennel seeds, coriander seeds, oregano, cumin, and salt. Pour in the beer and tomatoes. Stir well to evenly distribute the flavours. Nestle in the beef shank and cover tightly. Place in the oven and slowly braise, turning the meat once an hour, until tender, 3 hours. Remove from the oven and let the shank rest in the Dutch oven at room temperature for at least 2 hours. (You can prepare the shank to this point, leave in the liquid, tightly cover, and refrigerate for up to 5 days before continuing.)

BUILD A FIRE

Build and tend an active fire in your firepit, with a growing bed of glowing hot coals to one side. Position a grill grate over the fire and a large cast-iron skillet over the coals next to the active fire. Alternatively, light your charcoal grill or fire up your gas grill to its highest setting.

GRILL THE POBLANO PEPPERS AND MAKE THE SALSA

Position the poblano peppers on the grate and grill, turning frequently, until lightly charred and softened. Transfer to a plate and let rest until cool enough to handle. Slice each poblano lengthwise and carefully remove and discard the stem, seeds, and pith. Finely dice the peppers. In a serving bowl, stir together the diced peppers, tomatoes, cilantro, lime zest and juice, salt, and minced sriracha pickled red onions. Reserve or transfer to a resealable container and refrigerate overnight.

SEAR THE BEEF SHANK

Carefully transfer the tender beef shank from the braising liquid to the hot cast-iron skillet. Sear with both the direct heat of the cast iron below and the adjacent heat of the active fire to the side.

Meanwhile, skim and discard most of the fat from the liquid in the Dutch oven, season with the cider vinegar, place over the direct heat, and simmer until reduced by half. Discard the bay leaves.

Continue searing the beef shank, turning occasionally and basting with the simmering braising liquid, until charred and heated through, 20 minutes or so. Remove from the heat. With a pair of metal tongs and a fork, pull, tug, and shred the meat from the bone. Stir into the reduced sauce.

ASSEMBLE THE TACOS

Lightly toast the tortillas over the fire. Fill the tortillas with braised beef shank, fresh salsa with cilantro and lime, a few sriracha pickled red onions, and a sprig of cilantro.

SERVES 12

SPECIAL EQUIPMENT NEEDED: large cast-iron Dutch oven; large cast-iron skillet

BRAISED AND CHARRED BEEF SHANK

2 large yellow or white onions, thinly sliced

Cloves from 1 head of garlic, thinly sliced

5 dried guajillo chilies, stem and seeds discarded, broken or cut into small pieces

5 dried ancho chilies, stem and seeds discarded, broken or cut into small pieces

2 bay leaves

1 tablespoon (15 mL) fennel seeds

1 tablespoon (15 mL) coriander seeds

1 tablespoon (15 mL) dried oregano

1 tablespoon (15 mL) ground cumin

1 tablespoon (15 mL) sea salt

2 bottles (12 ounces/354 mL each) light Mexican beer

1 can (28 ounces/796 mL) crushed tomatoes

1 bone-in beef shank (4 pounds/1.8 kg)

1 tablespoon (15 mL) apple cider vinegar

GRILLED CHILI SALSA

4 poblano peppers or New Mexican–style chili peppers

2 pounds (900 g) ripe tomatoes, finely diced

Leaves and tender stems from 1 bunch of fresh cilantro, chopped, a few sprigs reserved for garnish

Zest and juice of 4 limes

1 teaspoon (5 mL) sea salt

¼ cup (60 mL) minced Sriracha Pickled Red Onions (page 258)

FOR THE TACOS

24 flour or corn tortillas (page 71 for flour tortillas)

Sriracha Pickled Red Onions (page 258)

REVERSE SEARING
Cooking Method

Braising and tenderizing meat before searing the surface to develop flavour and texture. Classically, meat is seared and then braised, but the reverse method allows the cook to add delicious texture to the dish by carefully charring the finished tender meat.

CHICKEN SHAWARMA WITH
CUCUMBER DILL TZATZIKI

Classic street food flavours from the Middle East. Deliciously marinated chicken thighs, slowly roasted on an ingenious vertical rig, then pita-rolled with a bright half-salad/half-sauce tzatziki. This is a spectacular showpiece for your next fireside party, with authentic flavours and slow, patient sharing built into the method.

MARINATE THE CHICKEN

In a large bowl, whisk together the yogurt, lemon zest and juice, garlic, paprika, cumin, oregano, chili flakes, salt, and cinnamon. Add the chicken and toss until evenly mixed. Cover tightly and refrigerate overnight.

MAKE THE CUCUMBER DILL TZATZIKI

In a medium bowl, whisk together the yogurt, garlic, lemon zest and juice, dill, and salt. Grate the cucumbers through the large holes of a box grater. Use your hands to squeeze out as much excess moisture as you can before adding to the yogurt mixture. Stir together, cover tightly, and refrigerate until needed.

BUILD A FIRE

Build and tend an active fire in your firepit, bringing to high heat with live flame and a growing bed of glowing hot coals. Create an offset roasting zone against a reflective wall next to the fire, using stacked cinder blocks. Alternatively, tend the fire to medium heat and position a horizontal rotisserie rig directly above the heat (see page 46).

SKEWER THE SHAWARMA AND SLOWLY ROAST

Fit the vertical skewer to its pan base. Spear an onion half on the skewer, cut side down. One at a time, skewer the chicken thighs onto the skewer, layering each thigh at 90 degrees to the previous one so they are spread evenly around the skewer, forming an even roast-shaped mass. Top with the remaining onion half, cut side down. Alternatively, thread the chicken onto a rotisserie spit, omitting the onion halves.

Place the chicken-stuffed rig in the roasting zone. Roast, turning frequently, evenly exposing all sides to the indirect heat, until the surface is browned and lightly charred and an instant-read thermometer inserted to a depth of an inch (2.5 cm) or more registers 165°F (74°C), 2 hours or so. Juices will accumulate in the pan; when they begin to sizzle and brown, pour in the water and frequently spoon the juices over the roasting meat. To carve, steady the top of the skewer with one hand, and with the other slice the golden roast chicken from the entire surface, exposing the inside to finishing heat.

Briefly warm each pita over the fire before stuffing. Cut a slit in one edge of the pita and open halfway, folding back the top. Smear the inside of the pocket with a heaping spoonful of cucumber dill tzatziki and fill with sliced chicken. Top with sliced red onion, diced tomato, and olives. Garnish with the reserved dill sprigs. Roll tightly and share individually or cut into rounds and share with a crowd.

SERVES 12 TO 16

SPECIAL EQUIPMENT NEEDED: vertical spit and roasting pan; masonry or metal reflective wall behind and above the fire; digital instant-read thermometer

MARINATED CHICKEN

2 cups (500 mL) natural plain full-fat yogurt or plain Greek yogurt

Zest and juice of 1 lemon

4 garlic cloves, finely grated with a microplane or finely minced

2 tablespoons (30 mL) paprika

2 tablespoons (30 mL) ground cumin

2 tablespoons (30 mL) dried oregano

1 tablespoon (15 mL) red chili flakes

1 tablespoon (15 mL) sea salt

1 teaspoon (5 mL) cinnamon

4 pounds (1.8 kg) skinless, boneless chicken thighs

1 large yellow or white onion, peeled, halved crosswise

½ cup (125 mL) water

CUCUMBER DILL TZATZIKI

2 cups (500 mL) natural plain full-fat yogurt or plain Greek yogurt

2 large garlic cloves

Zest and juice of 2 lemons

Leaves and tender stems from 1 large bunch of fresh dill, minced, a few sprigs reserved for garnish

1 teaspoon (5 mL) sea salt

8 Persian-style cucumbers

FOR SERVING

12 to 16 fresh pitas

1 large red onion, thinly sliced

2 or 3 large ripe tomatoes, diced

1 cup (250 mL) Kalamata olives, pitted and halved

VERTICAL SPIT
Classic Cooking Tool

A simple way of skewering ingredients onto a supportive centre rod above a moisture-collecting pan, improvising a uniform mass ready for even cooking by slowly rotating next to or above a fire. Because the outer layer browns first, it is usually sliced away and enjoyed while the inner layers continue to cook.

IRON SEAFOOD CHOWDER

We've made thousands of batches of our signature chowder and not one has ever burned. Our secret is our classic cast-iron Dutch ovens. We honour the sea around us and the regional heritage of this classic soup with attention to every detail. Impeccable ingredients patiently crafted. A flavourful fish broth is simmered first so the delicate shellfish can be stirred in last. We season with the natural brininess of shellfish juices and salt cod, wait for nothing but the starch of the simmering potatoes to thicken the works, and finish with fresh cream and fragrant parsley. We believe chowder should be served freshly made and fiercely hot, so we ladle ours still simmering into preheated mini cast-iron pots.

MAKE THE CHOWDER BROTH

In a large pot over medium-high heat, combine the fish bones, onion, carrot, celery, bay leaves, thyme, milk, salt, and pepper. Bring to a slow, steady simmer and cook for 30 minutes. Remove from the heat, cover tightly, and let rest for 30 minutes. Strain through a mesh strainer set over another large pot or bowl. Discard the solids. The broth can be covered tightly and refrigerated for up to 5 days or frozen for up to 3 months.

SOAK THE SALT COD

In a small bowl, break the salt cod into a few pieces. Add the milk, cover tightly with plastic wrap, and refrigerate for at least 2 hours or overnight. Drain well, discarding the salty milk. Flake the salt cod into smaller pieces.

BUILD A FIRE

Build and tend an active fire in your firepit, bringing to medium-high heat with live flame and a growing bed of glowing hot coals. Position a grill grate directly over the fire. As you cook the chowder, the fire will die down through the heat zones you need.

MAKE THE CHOWDER

Set a large cast-iron Dutch oven or large soup pot on the grill grate and toss in the bacon and a splash of water. Cook, stirring frequently, until sizzling hot and lightly crisped but not browned, about 5 minutes. Add the onion, carrot, and celery and cook without browning, stirring frequently, just until the vegetables are sizzling bright and fragrant, 3 or 4 minutes.

SERVES 6 TO 8

SPECIAL EQUIPMENT NEEDED: large cast-iron Dutch oven

CHOWDER BROTH

2 pounds (900 g) white fish bones or unpeeled frozen shrimp

1 large yellow onion, thinly sliced

1 large carrot, peeled and thinly sliced

1 celery stalk, thinly sliced

2 bay leaves

4 sprigs of fresh thyme

4 cups (1 L) whole milk or water

1 teaspoon (5 mL) sea salt

Freshly ground black pepper

MARITIME CHOWDER

6 ounces (170 g) salt cod

2 cups (500 mL) whole milk

4 slices bacon, cut crosswise into thin strips

1 large yellow onion, finely diced

1 large carrot, peeled and finely diced

1 celery stalk, finely diced

½ cup (125 mL) dry white wine

5 pounds (2.25 kg) fresh mussels, rinsed well and beards removed

1 jar (5 ounces/153 g) bar clams, chopped, juices reserved

4 cups (1 L) Chowder Broth (recipe above) or whole milk

2 Yukon Gold or baking potatoes, peeled and cut into ½-inch (1 cm) cubes

1 cup (250 mL) heavy (35%) cream

Meat from 2 cooked lobsters, chopped

6 ounces (170 g) scallops

6 ounces (170 g) crab meat, carefully picked over for any bits of shell

6 ounces (170 g) fresh white fish (such as halibut, hake, haddock)

1 dozen impeccably fresh Prince Edward Island oysters from a well-connected fishmonger, carefully shucked to retain the juices

1 cup (250 mL) minced fresh curly or flat-leaf parsley

1 bunch of fresh chives, thinly sliced

Recipe continues

Pour in the white wine and add the mussels. Cover tightly with a lid and steam until all the shells open and the meat within is cooked through, 5 minutes or so. Remove the pot from the heat and discard any mussels that did not open. Remove the meat from the shells and reserve. Discard the shells.

To the pot add the reserved clam juice, chowder broth, potatoes, and reserved salt cod. Bring to a simmer and cook until the potatoes are tender, 10 to 15 minutes. Add the cream and return to a simmer.

Stir in the lobster, scallops, crab meat, white fish, and reserved clams and mussel meat. Return to a full simmer and cook just until the fish is heated through, 2 or 3 minutes. Remove from the heat. Stir in the oysters, parsley, and chives. Ladle into individual serving bowls and share with your favourite biscuits. Leftovers can be covered tightly and refrigerated for up to 3 days before a thorough reheating.

CAST-IRON DUTCH OVEN
Essential Fire Kitchen Tool

Heavy-duty cast iron captures, retains, and evenly transfers the high heat of live flame to food. A properly seasoned vessel is perfectly non-stick, is easy to care for, and will last for generations. A cast-iron Dutch oven retains heat so well that it can rest in front of the fire, next to the heat rather than above it, and still draw enough cooking heat.

WOOD OVEN–FIRED PIZZA

There are many ways to make great-tasting pizza but only a powerfully built wood oven produces the intense retained heat that quickly cooks and deliciously chars this simple classic. This is how we craft our version of the old-world pizza that tops them all.

BUILD A FIRE

Build a steady active fire in your wood oven, tending for several days as needed to fill the thermal mass with retained heat. Monitor the cooking temperature with a high-temperature ovenproof thermometer or surface thermometer. Tend the fire, bringing the oven floor to at least 700°F (378°C). Before baking, push all the live fire embers into a tight pile in the back corner of the oven, leaving a large, clear baking area. Brush and clean the baking surface with a dedicated wet oven mop.

MAKE THE PIZZA DOUGH

Measure the warm water into a large bowl. Sprinkle the yeast over the water and let rest until dissolved, 2 or 3 minutes. Stir in the salt and olive oil. Add the flour and with the handle of a wooden spoon mix well until the ingredients are fully incorporated and a rough dough forms. Lightly flour your hands and work surface. Turn out the dough and knead until smooth, 5 minutes or so. Cut the dough ball into 8 equal pieces. Place each ball in a resealable plastic sandwich or storage bag and refrigerate overnight. The long, slow rise makes the dough easier to handle and tastier.

LET THE DOUGH RISE

Remove the dough from the fridge. Line a baking sheet with parchment paper and dust lightly with flour. Lightly flour your hands, work surface, and the dough balls. Working with 1 piece of dough at a time, shape the dough into a smooth, firm ball, then let rest on the lined baking sheet, covered loosely with plastic wrap and a kitchen towel, in a warm spot until doubled in size, 30 minutes or so.

MAKE THE TOMATO SAUCE

Pour the tomatoes into a food processor. Position a microplane grater over the bowl and grate the garlic into a fine paste. Tap sharply to fully release the garlic purée into the tomatoes below. Add the olive oil and chili flakes and process until thoroughly puréed into a smooth sauce. Transfer to a medium bowl and reserve.

MAKES 8 MEDIUM PIZZAS, ENOUGH FOR A PARTY OF 20, EASILY HALVED WITH LEFTOVER SAUCE

SPECIAL EQUIPMENT NEEDED: wood oven; high-temperature ovenproof thermometer or surface thermometer; pizza peel; pizza cutter; oven mop; oven coal scraper

PIZZA DOUGH

3½ cups (875 mL) warm water
2 tablespoons (30 mL) active dry yeast
4 teaspoons (20 mL) sea salt
¼ cup (60 mL) extra-virgin olive oil
9 cups (2.25 L) all-purpose flour, plus more for dusting

TOMATO SAUCE

1 can (28 ounces/796 g) whole peeled San Marzano tomatoes
4 garlic cloves
1 tablespoon (15 mL) extra-virgin olive oil
1 teaspoon (5 mL) red chili flakes

FOR ASSEMBLY

Leaves from 1 large bunch of fresh basil
1 pound (450 g) fresh cow's or buffalo milk mozzarella, thinly sliced or shredded

Recipe continues

SHAPE THE DOUGH AND ASSEMBLE THE PIZZAS

When the dough has doubled in size, lightly flour your hands, work surface, pizza peel, and the dough balls. Working with 1 dough ball at a time, stretch, pull, and shape the dough into a thin disc with a raised edge, 10 inches (25 cm) or so across. Lift the dough onto a lightly floured peel and shake the peel gently to confirm it is not sticky. Practise your release snap before loading the dough with toppings.

Working quickly, using the back of a spoon, evenly spread 6 tablespoons (90 mL) of the tomato sauce in a thin layer across the surface of the dough, stopping about ½ inch (1 cm) or so from the edge. Cover the sauce with an eighth of the basil leaves. Sprinkle, lay, or crumble an eighth of the cheese across the surface. Repeat with the remaining pizzas.

BAKE THE PIZZAS

Just before building each pizza, add a piece of hardwood fuel to the embers, waiting for tongues of live flame to lick the ceiling of the wood oven before firing the pizza. This balances the intense retained heat in the oven floor with equally fierce heat above so the dough and toppings cook together. Pick up the peel and transfer to the floor of the wood oven at least 8 inches (20 cm) from the ember pile. Release the pizza with a quick reverse snap, allowing it to slide onto the hot surface. Bake, rotating once, until the bottom is golden brown, the edge crusty and lightly charred, and the cheese lightly browned and bubbling, 2 to 5 minutes. Often the first pie of any pizza baking rally is a calibration effort as the full heat of the oven reveals itself to the baker.

Use the pizza peel to transfer the pizzas to a cutting board. Slice each into 8 wedges. Let cool briefly. Serve with a fresh green salad.

RETAINED HEAT
Wood Oven Method

The intense steady heat built up over time within the thermal mass of a wood oven, the thousands of pounds of masonry and sand above the chamber and within its floor. The steady day-long release of heat after the live fire and embers have died down. Essential heat for baking bread, which cannot endure a live fire in the oven cavity.

SMOKED CHEDDAR WHOLE WHEAT PIZZA WITH APPLE OREGANO SAUCE

A classic pizza with some tasty tweaks. Whole wheat crust for hearty flavour. Pizza sauce made the way it's always made but with a different fruit, apples instead of tomatoes. Topped with salty country ham and mellow smoked cheddar.

BUILD A FIRE

Build a steady active fire in your wood oven, tending for several days as needed to fill the thermal mass with retained heat. Monitor the cooking temperature with a high-temperature ovenproof thermometer or surface thermometer. Tend the fire, bringing the oven floor to at least 700°F (378°C). Before baking, push all the live fire embers into a tight pile in the back corner of the oven, leaving a large, clear baking area. Brush and clean the baking surface with a dedicated wet oven mop.

MAKE THE PIZZA DOUGH

Measure the warm water into a large bowl. Sprinkle the yeast over the water and let rest until dissolved, 2 or 3 minutes. Stir in the salt and olive oil. Add the all-purpose and whole wheat flours and with the handle of a wooden spoon mix well until the ingredients are fully incorporated and a rough dough forms. Lightly flour your hands and work surface with all-purpose flour. Turn out the dough and knead until smooth, 5 minutes or so. Cut the ball into 4 equal pieces. Place each ball in a resealable plastic sandwich or storage bag and refrigerate overnight. The long, slow rise makes the dough easier to handle and tastier.

LET THE DOUGH RISE

Remove the dough from the fridge. Line a baking sheet with parchment paper and dust lightly with all-purpose flour. Lightly flour your hands, work surface, and the dough balls with all-purpose flour. Working with 1 piece of dough at a time, shape the dough into a smooth, firm ball, then let rest on the lined baking sheet, covered loosely with plastic wrap and a kitchen towel, in a warm spot until doubled in size, 30 minutes or so.

MEANWHILE, MAKE THE APPLE OREGANO SAUCE

Heat the olive oil in a medium saucepan over medium-high heat. Add the onion and garlic and sauté until sizzling and fragrant but not browned, 2 or 3 minutes. Stir in the oregano. Add the apples, white wine, salt, and pepper. Bring the mixture to a slow simmer and cook until the apples are very tender, 15 minutes or so. Purée until smooth with an immersion blender.

MAKES 4 MEDIUM PIZZAS, SERVES 4 AS A MEAL OR 8 AS A SNACK

SPECIAL EQUIPMENT NEEDED: wood oven; high-temperature ovenproof thermometer or surface thermometer; pizza peel; pizza cutter; oven mop; oven coal scraper

WHOLE WHEAT PIZZA DOUGH

1¾ cups (425 mL) warm water

1 tablespoon (15 mL) active dry yeast

2 teaspoons (10 mL) sea salt

2 tablespoons (30 mL) extra-virgin olive oil

3 cups (750 mL) all-purpose flour, plus more for dusting

1½ cups (375 mL) whole wheat flour

APPLE OREGANO SAUCE

1 tablespoon (15 mL) olive oil

1 large yellow onion, finely diced

6 garlic cloves, finely minced

1 teaspoon (5 mL) dried oregano

4 large Honeycrisp apples or your favourite variety, unpeeled, cored, cut into chunks

½ cup (125 mL) white wine

Sea salt

Freshly ground black pepper

FOR ASSEMBLY

6 ounces (170 g) thinly sliced country ham or prosciutto, rolled and cut into thin ribbons

12 ounces (340 g) smoked cheddar cheese, grated

Recipe continues

SHAPE THE DOUGH AND ASSEMBLE THE PIZZAS

When the dough has doubled in size, lightly flour your hands, work surface, pizza peel, and the dough balls with all-purpose flour. Working with 1 dough ball at a time, stretch, pull, and shape the dough into a thin disc with a raised edge, 10 inches (25 cm) or so across. Lift the dough onto a lightly floured peel and shake the peel gently to confirm it is not sticky. Practise your release snap before loading the dough with toppings.

Working quickly, using the back of a spoon, evenly spread a quarter of the apple oregano sauce across the surface of the dough, stopping about ½ inch (1 cm) or so from the edge. Sprinkle a quarter of the ham over the sauce and cover evenly with a quarter of the grated cheddar cheese. Repeat with the remaining pizzas.

BAKE THE PIZZAS

Just before building each pizza, add a piece of hardwood fuel to the embers, waiting for tongues of live flame to lick the ceiling of the wood oven before firing the pizza. This balances the intense retained heat in the oven floor with equally fierce heat above, so the dough and toppings cook together. Pick up the peel and transfer to the floor of the wood oven at least 8 inches (20 cm) from the ember pile. Release the pizza with a quick reverse snap, allowing it to slide onto the hot surface. Bake, rotating once, until the bottom is golden brown, the edge crusty and lightly charred, and the cheese lightly browned and bubbling, 2 to 5 minutes. Often the first pie of any pizza baking rally is a calibration effort as the full heat of the oven reveals itself to the baker.

Use the pizza peel to transfer the pizzas to a cutting board. Slice each into 8 wedges. Let cool briefly. Serve with a fresh green salad.

LIVE-FIRE OVEN
Wood Oven Method

Cooking within the enclosed cavity of a wood oven with the reflected heat of a live fire. Classically, pizza crusts are baked from beneath with the heat retained in the oven masonry from days of firing, while the pizza toppings are cooked from above by the flames of a live fire licking the roof of the oven. Live fire is also a way to bring a wood oven online quickly without waiting for the retained heat to build.

GRILLED PIZZA WITH FRESH BASIL, HEIRLOOM TOMATOES, AND MOZZARELLA

A tasty improvised way to flavour a wood-fired grilling party with traditional pizza ingredients and a perfectly suited cooking method. Classic pizza dough baked and toasted first, aromatic basil, fragrant tomatoes, and fresh mozzarella.

MAKE THE PIZZA DOUGH

Measure the warm water into a large bowl. Sprinkle the yeast over the water and let rest until dissolved, 2 or 3 minutes. Stir in the salt and olive oil. Add the flour and with the handle of a wooden spoon mix well until the ingredients are fully incorporated and a rough dough forms. Lightly flour your hands and work surface. Turn out the dough and knead until smooth, 5 minutes or so. Cut the ball into 4 equal pieces. Place each ball in a resealable plastic sandwich or storage bag and refrigerate overnight. The long, slow rise makes the dough easier to handle and tastier.

LET THE DOUGH RISE

Remove the dough from the fridge. Line a baking sheet with parchment paper and dust lightly with flour. Lightly flour your hands, work surface, and the dough balls. Working with 1 piece of dough at a time, shape the dough into a smooth, firm ball, then let rest on the lined baking sheet, covered loosely with plastic wrap and a kitchen towel, in a warm spot until doubled in size, 30 minutes or so.

MEANWHILE, MAKE THE BASIL PURÉE

Add the basil to a food processor. Position a microplane grater over the bowl and grate the garlic into a fine paste. Tap sharply to fully release the garlic purée into the basil below. Add the olive oil, chili flakes, and salt. Process into a smooth purée. Transfer to a small bowl and reserve.

BUILD A FIRE

Build a wood or charcoal fire in your Big Green Egg, tending it past active flame to a glowing bed of hot coals and medium-high heat. Position a grill grate directly over the fire. Lightly oil the grate. Alternatively, fire up your gas grill or covered barbecue.

SHAPE THE DOUGH

When the dough has doubled in size, lightly flour your hands, work surface, and the dough balls. Working with 1 dough ball at a time, stretch, pull, and shape the dough into a thin disc with a raised edge, 10 inches (25 cm) or so across.

Recipe continues

MAKES 4 MEDIUM PIZZAS, SERVES 4 AS A MEAL OR 8 AS A SNACK

SPECIAL EQUIPMENT NEEDED: Big Green Egg, other ceramic kamado-style grill, or covered gas grill or barbecue

NEAPOLITAN-STYLE PIZZA DOUGH

1¾ cups (425 mL) warm water

1 tablespoon (15 mL) active dry yeast

2 teaspoons (10 mL) sea salt

2 tablespoons (30 mL) extra-virgin olive oil

4½ cups (1.1 L) all-purpose flour, plus more for dusting

BASIL PURÉE

Leaves and tender stems from 2 large bunches of fresh basil

4 garlic cloves

½ cup (125 mL) extra-virgin olive oil

1 teaspoon (5 mL) red chili flakes

1 teaspoon (5 mL) sea salt

FOR ASSEMBLY

4 large vine-ripened heirloom tomatoes, thinly sliced

8 ounces (225 g) fresh cow's or buffalo milk mozzarella, thinly sliced or crumbled

GRILL THE PIZZA DOUGH

Use your hands to lift the stretched dough directly onto the grill grates over the highest heat. Cook just long enough to lightly char and tightly seal the bottom, a minute or so. Flip over and cook just long enough to char and seal the second side. Remove from the grill.

ASSEMBLE AND FINISH GRILLING THE PIZZA

Working quickly, using the back of a spoon, evenly spread ¼ cup (60 mL) of basil purée across the surface of the dough, stopping about ½ inch (1 cm) or so from the edge. Cover the sauce with a single layer of sliced tomatoes. Top with fresh mozzarella. Return to the grill, close the lid, and continue cooking until the crust is browned, the toppings heated, and the cheese melted, another minute or so. Repeat with the remaining pizzas.

Transfer the pizzas to a cutting board. Slice each into 8 wedges. Let cool briefly. Serve with a fresh green salad.

GRILLING PIZZA
Outdoor Cooking Method

A cooking technique that harnesses the heat of a grill to approximate the flavourful charring effect of a pizza oven. Grilling and cooking the fresh pizza dough first before adding finishing sauce and toppings and heating again.

WOOD-FIRED
BEEF CLASSICS

WOOD-GRILLED CHEF'S STEAK WITH JALAPEÑO CHIMICHURRI

There are many steaks beyond classic loin cuts, each with their own distinctive flavour and texture. Flatiron is an intensely beefy steak cut from the shoulder, the second-most tender part of a cow after the tenderloin. The meat is well marbled, very tender, and relatively inexpensive. Perhaps that's why so many chefs and butchers consider it their favourite steak, especially grilled over a wood fire and served with the sharp, fragrant accent of classic chimichurri.

MAKE THE JALAPEÑO CHIMICHURRI

In a food processor, combine the onion, jalapeño, garlic, red wine vinegar, and olive oil and process until smooth. Add the oregano, paprika, cumin, salt, parsley, and water. Process until the parsley is finely chopped. Transfer to a small bowl, cover, and let rest so the flavours have a chance to develop, at least a few hours or overnight. Refrigerate any leftovers in a resealable container for up to 1 month.

BUILD A FIRE

Build and tend an active fire in your firepit, bringing to medium-high heat with some active flame and a growing bed of glowing hot coals. Position a grill grate directly over the fire. Lightly oil the grate. Alternatively, light your charcoal grill or fire up your gas grill to its highest setting.

SEASON THE STEAK

Place the steak on a wire rack over a baking sheet. Pat dry with paper towel. Evenly season each side with 1 teaspoon (5 mL) of the coarse salt. Cover and let rest at room temperature as the seasoning finds its way into the meat, at least 1 hour but no more than 2 hours. Season with lots of coarsely ground pepper just before cooking. Clean the rack.

GRILL THE STEAK

Sear the steak over medium high heat, turning occasionally, until charred, about 5 minutes per side for medium-rare. Transfer the finished steak to the rack, brush with soft butter, and let rest in a warm place near the fire for 10 minutes or so. Thinly slice the steak against the grain. Spoon some of the jalapeño chimichurri over the meat and serve the rest on the side.

SERVES 4 TO 6

JALAPEÑO CHIMICHURRI

1 medium white or yellow onion, peeled and quartered

1 jalapeño pepper, peeled, halved, stem, seeds, and pith discarded

Cloves from 1 head of garlic, peeled

¼ cup (60 mL) red wine vinegar

¼ cup (60 mL) extra-virgin olive oil

2 tablespoons (30 mL) dried oregano

1 tablespoon (15 mL) smoked paprika

1 teaspoon (5 mL) ground cumin

1 teaspoon (5 mL) sea salt

Leaves and tender stems from 1 bunch of fresh flat-leaf or curly parsley

¼ cup (60 mL) water

GRILLED FLATIRON STEAK

1 flatiron steak (2 pounds/900 g) or your favourite grilling steak

2 teaspoons (10 mL) coarse sea salt or kosher salt

Coarsely ground black pepper

2 tablespoons (30 mL) salted butter, at room temperature

CHEF'S STEAK
Secret Ingredient

Traditionally, the tenderness and thus high value of beef loin steaks meant they were reserved for paying guests while the butcher and chef relied on less valuable cuts to feed their families. A vast repertoire of delicious cuts awaits the adventurous palate, and fire chefs know the cooking peculiarities of each one: flatiron, flank, hanger, skirt, bavette, picanha, and tri-tip.

WOOD-GRILLED SALT AND PEPPER RIBEYE STEAKS WITH MAÎTRE D'HOTEL BUTTER

When you take the time to cut down a tree, block it, split it, stack it, wait two years, build a fire, and wait an hour for the perfect heat, you naturally appreciate the best ingredients. Like many chefs, I'll forever crave the extravagant ribeye's perfect balance of beefy flavour, contrasting texture, and juiciness—the crown jewel of beef elevated with wood-fired cooking, embellished simply with salt and pepper, and maître d'hotel, the traditional flavoured butter of continental hotel dining rooms and classic steakhouses, gently melting with the juices of the steak into a deliciously improvised sauce.

MAKE THE MAÎTRE D'HOTEL BUTTER

In a medium bowl, stir together the butter, horseradish, shallots, garlic, anchovies, tarragon, lemon zest and juice, and pepper until evenly mixed.

Lightly moisten a work surface with water to aid adhesion. Lay an 18-inch (46 cm) piece of plastic wrap over the surface with a long side facing you. Scoop the butter along the long edge closest to you, forming an even log shape about 8 inches (20 cm) long. Roll the butter once so it is encased in the plastic wrap, press into an even shape, then tightly roll up. Grasp the ends of the plastic and twirl the works a few times, tightening the butter into a perfect round log. Refrigerate or freeze until the butter is firm enough to slice, several hours, even overnight. A few minutes before serving, without removing the plastic wrap, cut into ¼-inch (5 mm) thick rounds. Unwind and discard the thin strip of plastic wrap around each slice and reserve the rounds on a small plate at room temperature.

SEASON THE STEAKS

Place the steaks on a wire rack over a baking sheet. Pat dry with paper towel. Evenly season both sides with the coarse salt. Cover and let rest at room temperature as the seasoning finds its way into the meat, at least 1 hour but no more than 2. Season with lots of freshly ground black pepper just before cooking.

BUILD A FIRE

Build and tend an active fire in your firepit, bring to high heat with live flame and a growing bed of glowing hot coals. Position a lightly oiled grill grate directly over the fire. Alternatively, light your charcoal grill or fire up your gas grill to its highest setting.

GRILL THE STEAKS

Lightly oil the grill grate. Sear the steaks over the high heat, turning and flipping occasionally, until browned, tender, and cooked to your liking, 10 minutes or so. Serve topped with a thick slice of maître d'hotel butter.

SERVES 4, WITH LEFTOVER MAÎTRE D'HOTEL BUTTER

MAÎTRE D'HOTEL BUTTER

1 pound (450 g) salted butter, softened
2 tablespoons (30 mL) prepared horseradish or Dijon mustard
4 shallots, finely minced
4 garlic cloves, finely minced
4 anchovy fillets, finely minced
Leaves and tender stems from 1 bunch of fresh tarragon, finely chopped
Zest and juice of 1 lemon
Lots of freshly ground black pepper

WOOD-GRILLED RIBEYE STEAKS

4 (1-inch/2.5 cm thick) ribeye steaks (about 4 pounds/1.8 kg total)
4 teaspoons (20 mL) coarse sea salt or kosher salt
Lots of freshly ground black pepper

COMPOUND BUTTER
Fire Kitchen Ingredient

Fresh butter flavoured with a variety of savoury flavours and aromatic herbs, rolled into a log, chilled until firm, then sliced into thick rounds that easily melt over a just-grilled steak into a tasty sauce. A freezer staple awaiting an improvised steak dinner.

EMBER-ROASTED CAVEMAN RIBEYE STEAKS WITH BOARD SAUCE

Thick, beefy steaks primally seared directly on the glowing embers of an active fire. A fireside sauce cleverly improvised from the meat resting over an aromatic paste of fresh herbs, its juices mingling with the bright flavours.

SEASON THE STEAKS

Pat the steaks dry with paper towel. Place on a resting platter. Evenly season both sides of the ribeyes with the salt. Cover and let rest at room temperature as the seasoning finds its way into the meat, at least 1 hour but no more than 2.

BUILD A FIRE

Build and tend a hardwood fire in your firepit, bringing to a glowing bed of fiercely hot active coals. Stir the embers to knock off the active wood ash. Form into an even glowing bed, about 16 inches (40 cm) square and 6 inches (15 cm) thick.

PREP THE BOARD SAUCE

Pile the shallot, garlic, and fresh herbs on a cutting board. Sprinkle with salt and pepper. Mince and mash, making a rough paste. Smear into a 6-inch (15 cm) square, awaiting the finished steaks.

EMBER-ROAST THE STEAKS

Vigorously fan the glowing embers to blow away any accumulated ash. Season the steaks with lots of pepper and immediately position them directly on the hot ash-free coals. Sear, turning occasionally, caramelizing the surface and roasting the steaks. The meat-covered coals lose temperature, so to maintain maximum heat, occasionally move the steak to a new part of the coal bed and allow the previous spot to rebuild its heat. As you turn the meat, brush off any bits of charcoal that stick. Continue cooking until an instant-read thermometer registers 135° to 140°F (57° to 60°C) for the perfect balance of juiciness, texture, and colour, 10 minutes or so.

Transfer the steaks to the herb paste on the cutting board. Brush with melted butter and let rest in a warm place near the fire for 10 minutes before slicing. Slice against the grain and toss together with the accumulated juices and warm herb paste. Serve with an array of sides and salads.

SERVES 4 TO 6

SPECIAL EQUIPMENT NEEDED: digital instant-read thermometer; large wooden cutting board

CAVEMAN RIBEYE STEAKS

2 (1- to 1½-inch/2.5 to 4 cm thick) bone-in ribeye steaks (about 2 pounds/900 g total)

2 teaspoons (10 mL) coarse sea salt or kosher salt

Lots of freshly ground black pepper

2 tablespoons (30 mL) salted butter, melted

BOARD SAUCE

1 shallot, finely minced

2 garlic cloves, finely minced

Leaves and tender stems from a few sprigs of fresh flat-leaf or curly parsley

A handful of fresh chives, thinly sliced

Leaves and tender stems from a few sprigs of fresh thyme, tarragon, or sage

½ teaspoon (2 mL) kosher salt

Freshly ground black pepper

EMBER ROASTING
Traditional Cooking Method

Cooking directly on or in the ash-free and smoke-free glowing coals of a hardwood fire, searing and roasting in the intense initial heat of the coals. An ancient cooking method to efficiently utilize the full heat of a hardwood fire. Flavourful smoke is generated by the meat's juices mingling with the heated coals.

BOARD SAUCE
Traditional Fireside Method

An improvised sauce formed by mingling the accumulating juices of a sizzling hot resting steak with a bright fresh herb paste.

IRON BEEF STEW WITH FARMHOUSE VEGETABLES

A classic beef and vegetable stew deeply flavoured through the versatility of cast-iron cookware—a thorough high-heat browning first before a long, patient simmer. Temperature extremes and a bright last-second greens finish.

BUILD A FIRE

Build and tend an active fire in your firepit, bringing to medium-high heat with live flame and a growing bed of glowing hot coals. Position a grill grate directly over the fire. Alternatively, light your charcoal grill or fire up your gas grill to its highest setting. Place a large cast-iron Dutch oven over the fire, preheating it to 500°F (260°C) or more. For best results use a surface thermometer.

SEAR THE BEEF

In a large bowl, toss together the beef, grapeseed oil, and salt. When the Dutch oven is very hot, carefully add the meat all at once and sear, stirring constantly with a wooden spoon, until all the pieces are deeply and evenly browned, 5 minutes or so.

SIMMER THE STEW

Pour in the red wine, dislodging the browned bits and reducing the Dutch oven's heat. Stir in the beef broth, tomatoes, onions, carrots, garlic, potatoes, bay leaves, thyme, and pepper. Bring to a slow, steady simmer, adjusting the position of the Dutch oven as needed. Cover tightly and cook, stirring occasionally, until the beef and vegetables are meltingly tender, about 2 hours. Taste and adjust seasoning as needed. Discard the bay leaves.

Fill each bowl with a handful of spinach. Top with a steaming ladleful of stew. Serve with an array of sides and salads.

SERVES 4 TO 6

SPECIAL EQUIPMENT NEEDED:
large cast-iron Dutch oven; surface thermometer

2 pounds (900 g) stewing beef, cut into 1-inch (2.5 cm) cubes

2 tablespoons (30 mL) grapeseed oil or rendered beef fat

1 teaspoon (5 mL) sea salt

1 bottle (26 ounces/750 mL) of your favourite big, bold red wine

4 cups (1 L) beef broth or water

1 can (28 ounces/796 mL) diced tomatoes

2 large yellow or white onions, cut into bite-size chunks

2 large carrots, peeled and cut into ½-inch (1 cm) thick rounds

Cloves from 1 head of garlic, halved

2 pounds (900 g) of your favourite potatoes, unpeeled, washed, cut into bite-size chunks

2 bay leaves

4 sprigs of fresh thyme

Freshly ground black pepper

10 ounces (280 g) baby spinach

IRON SEARING
Cast-Iron Cooking Method

Using the intense retained heat of a classic cast-iron Dutch oven to quickly and thoroughly sear stew meat, adding essential browned flavour with high heat before tenderly braising with very low heat.

SMASH CHEESEBURGERS

The classic griddle burger of the roadside diner perfected with the high heat of a cast-iron plancha. Rich, fatty ground chuck seared so quickly that the outside crisps before the inside overcooks, yielding an impossibly delicious blend of seared steak and beefy juiciness. Rolls toasted with heat-tolerant mayonnaise, yet another grill cook's secret.

FORM THE BURGERS

Divide the ground beef into 4 equal portions (about 5 ounces/140 g each). Using your hands, press and roll each portion into an even ball. Handle the meat as gently as possible to help it stay tender and juicy. Cover tightly with plastic wrap and refrigerate until ready to cook.

BUILD A FIRE

Build and tend an active fire in your firepit, bringing to medium-high heat with live flame and a growing bed of glowing hot coals. Position a seasoned cast-iron plancha or extra-large cast-iron skillet directly over the fire. Monitor the cooking temperature with a surface thermometer or infrared thermometer. Tend the fire and bring the plancha to 500°F (260°C) or so.

TOAST AND PREP THE BUNS

Lightly and evenly spread the cut sides of the buns with mayonnaise, about 1 teaspoon (5 mL) each bun. Position the bun halves mayonnaise side down on the plancha and briefly toast until golden brown and lightly crisped, just a minute or so. Transfer to a tray. Squeeze a swirl of yellow mustard on the bottom halves. Prep the tops with a swirl of ketchup and layer with lettuce, tomatoes, red onion, and pickles.

SMASH THE BURGERS

Just before cooking, generously season the meat balls with salt and pepper. Gently place the meat balls on the hot plancha, 6 inches (15 cm) or so apart. Balance a handful of sliced yellow onion on top of each ball. Using a wide metal spatula, press the onions firmly into the meat, forming a thin patty about 4 inches (10 cm) wide and ½ inch (1 cm) thick, with an irregular craggy edge. Cook, undisturbed, until the edges are sizzling brown and crispy and the base is seared, 2 minutes or so. Flip with the spatula, tucking any loose onions under the meat. Cover with a cheese slice and continue cooking until the meat is cooked through, another minute or two. Immediately transfer the burger to the mustard-ready bun bases with all the juices and flavour you can scrape from the plancha to soak into the toasted bun.

Cover the burgers with the bun tops with their salad toppings.

SERVES 4

SPECIAL EQUIPMENT NEEDED: large cast-iron plancha or extra-large cast-iron skillet; surface thermometer or infrared thermometer

SMASH CHEESEBURGERS

1¼ pounds (565 g) coarse-ground regular or medium-fat beef chuck

1 medium yellow onion, very thinly sliced on a mandoline

Kosher salt

Freshly ground black pepper

4 slices American-style cheese

BURGER BUILD

4 soft burger buns, split

Mayonnaise

Yellow mustard

Ketchup

4 large leaves Bibb lettuce

1 large ripe beefsteak tomato, thinly sliced

1 red onion, thinly sliced

8 dill pickle slices

PLANCHA SEARING
Cast-Iron Cooking Method

Utilizing the extremely high heat-retention ability of a cast-iron plancha over a roaring fire to sear at very high temperatures for maximum flavour. Fire and iron creating high-heat possibilities unavailable on normal gas and electric kitchen gear.

WOOD CANDLE STEAK WITH MUSHROOM AND ONION PAN SAUCE

Cooking and sharing food outdoors is one of life's great rewards, but try it once or twice and you quickly realize the logistical challenges of carrying heavy wood only to see most of the generated heat disappear. Here's how to transform a single block of well-seasoned wood and a simple cast-iron skillet into an efficiently concentrated heat source and a lifetime of flavours and stories.

SEASON THE STEAK

Pat dry the steak with paper towel. Place the steak on a resting platter. Evenly season the steak all over with the salt. Cover and let rest at room temperature as the seasoning finds its way into the meat, at least 1 hour but no more than 2.

BUILD A FIRE

Construct a wood candle (see page 53) from a full block (about 16 inches/ 40 cm tall and 12 inches/30 cm wide) of well-seasoned softwood or hardwood. Chainsaw two perpendicular cuts through the top face, forming a cross, cutting two-thirds of the way down the log, leaving a solid supportive base. Stuff tinder into the bottom of one slot and ignite with a match. Alternatively, direct a blowtorch flame through the bottom of a slot until the centre ignites. Patiently allow the exposed interior faces to fully ignite and begin burning from the centre, creating a fierce inner heat, 20 minutes or so. Place two small lengths of rebar on top to support the pan and maximize the heat flow beneath it. Preheat a large cast-iron skillet over the steel rods and the fire's heat.

PAN-ROAST THE STEAK AND MAKE THE PAN SAUCE

Season the steak with lots of pepper. Splash the grapeseed oil into the hot skillet. Carefully add the steak fat side down and sear, rendering its fat, keeping the pan at high sizzling heat, until lightly browned, 5 minutes or so. Turn the steak to one side of the pan and continue searing. When the second side has browned, fill the other side of the pan with the mushrooms and onions. Continue cooking the steak, turning occasionally, until browned on all sides, another 10 minutes or so. Stir the vegetables frequently as they absorb the steak's caramelized juices. The beef is done when an instant-read thermometer registers 120°F (50°C). Move the pan to a warm place near the fire. Lift the steak out of the pan for a moment while you add the wine and thyme and stir them into the mushrooms and onions. Bring to a simmer for a minute or so. Taste and adjust seasoning. Nestle the steak on top of the mixture, cover loosely with a square of folded foil, and let rest for 10 minutes before slicing.

SPECIAL EQUIPMENT NEEDED: full block of well-seasoned hardwood for cutting into a wood candle (see page 53); two 8-inch (20 cm) lengths of rebar; sharp chainsaw; large cast-iron skillet; digital instant-read thermometer

WOOD CANDLE STEAK

1 (3-inch/8 cm thick) New York strip steak (about 1½ pounds/675 g), fat cap trimmed to ½ inch (1 cm)
Kosher salt
Freshly ground black pepper
1 tablespoon (15 mL) grapeseed or vegetable oil

MUSHROOM AND ONION PAN SAUCE

1 pound (450 g) assorted wild or cultivated mushrooms, tougher stalks trimmed, halved, quartered, or sliced into bite-size pieces
1 large onion, thinly sliced
½ cup (125 mL) red wine (any type)
Leaves and tender stems from a few sprigs of fresh thyme, rosemary, or sage, minced
Kosher salt
Freshly ground black pepper

WOOD CANDLE
Outdoor Cooking Method

A genius bushcraft method perfected by the Swedish army to harness the most possible heat from the least possible wood. A standard block of seasoned wood transformed into both a stable cooking platform and a long-burning source of strong cooking heat. (See page 53.)

FLAME MIGNON WITH BLUE CHEESE TARRAGON BUTTER

Rich, tender filet mignon fully realized within the intense searing heat of live flame. A bland beef cut elevated by the wood fire. A delectable charred exterior roasted so quickly that the interior remains tender and juicy. An umami-rich butter gently melting and basting the resting meat with aromatic flavour.

MAKE THE BLUE CHEESE TARRAGON BUTTER
To a small food processor, add the butter, blue cheese, tarragon, and pepper. Purée into a smooth paste. Transfer to a small bowl and reserve.

BUILD A FIRE
Build and tend an active fire in your firepit. Stoke the fire, waiting for the wood to fully ignite into active roaring flames. Position a lightly oiled narrow-rod steel grill grate directly within the flames.

FLAME-ROAST THE STEAKS
Place the filet mignons on a baking sheet. Pat dry with paper towel. Evenly season each side with ½ teaspoon (2 mL) of salt and lots of pepper. Position the steaks on the grill within the fiercest flames of the fire and roast, turning constantly, searing and browning until charred and thoroughly roasted. The steaks are done when an instant-read thermometer registers 120°F (50°C).

Transfer the steaks to individual plates or a resting platter. Top each with a generous dollop of blue cheese tarragon butter and let rest in a warm place near the fire for 5 minutes before slicing.

SERVES 4

SPECIAL EQUIPMENT NEEDED: digital instant-read thermometer

BLUE CHEESE TARRAGON BUTTER
8 tablespoons (125 mL) salted butter, at room temperature

8 tablespoons (125 mL) traditional premium or artisanal blue cheese (Roquefort, Stilton, Gorgonzola, or Cabrales), at room temperature

Leaves and tender stems from 1 bunch of fresh tarragon, finely minced

½ teaspoon (2 mL) freshly ground black pepper

FILET MIGNON STEAKS
4 (2-inch/5 cm thick) filet mignon steaks (about 8 ounces/225 g each)

4 teaspoons (20 mL) sea salt

Freshly ground black pepper

FLAME ROASTING
Fire Cooking Method

Cooking an ingredient directly within the intensely hot flames of an active fire, quickly searing, roasting, and developing the flavour of the surface before transformative heat has a chance to penetrate farther.

WOOD-FIRED PORK, CHICKEN, AND LAMB

WOOD-ROASTED PORK LOIN WITH ROASTED SWEET POTATOES AND APPLES, AND WILTED ARUGULA

A thick pork loin roast patiently dry-brined, then slowly roasted to golden perfection over a thick bed of caramelized sweet potato and sour apples. Tangy arugula brings bright finishing balance to this memorable dish.

DRY-BRINE THE PORK LOIN
Place the roast on a wire rack over a baking sheet. Pat dry with paper towel. Evenly and liberally season the loin all over with the bay spice. Cover and let rest at room temperature as the seasoning finds its way into the meat, at least 1 hour but no more than 2.

BUILD A FIRE
Build and tend an active fire in your wood oven, bringing to medium roasting temperature and a bed of glowing hot coals. Push coals to the back, clearing a roasting area to the front. Monitor the cooking temperature with a high-temperature ovenproof thermometer or infrared thermometer. Tend the fire, bringing the oven to 350° to 400°F (180° to 200°C). Alternatively, preheat your indoor oven.

ROAST THE PORK LOIN AND VEGETABLES
Preheat a 16-inch (40 cm) cast-iron skillet in the wood oven. In a large bowl, toss together the sweet potatoes, apples, leeks, bacon fat, salt, and pepper. Remove the skillet from the oven and pour in the vegetable mixture. Nestle the pork loin skin side up in the middle of the pan. Nestle in the lemon halves cut side up. Return to the slower part of the oven and roast for about 1 hour, rotating the pan occasionally for even cooking, shaking and stirring now and then, until the vegetables are cooked and the meat is browned and tender. The pork is done when an instant-read thermometer in the thickest part of the meat registers 145°F (63°C). Remove the pan from the oven.

Transfer the pork roast to a resting plate. Squeeze the lemon halves over the vegetables. Add the arugula to the pan and stir gently to combine. Slice the pork and serve with lots of the roast veggies and wilted arugula.

SPECIAL EQUIPMENT NEEDED:
wood oven; 16-inch (40 cm) cast-iron skillet; high-temperature ovenproof thermometer or infrared thermometer; digital instant-read thermometer

WOOD-ROASTED PORK LOIN
1 bone-in pork loin roast (about 3 pounds/ 1.35 kg), fatty skin scored in a diamond pattern at ½-inch (1 cm) intervals
2 tablespoons (30 mL) Bay Spice (page 256)

ROASTED SWEET POTATOES AND APPLES
2 large sweet potatoes, peeled and cut into bite-size cubes
4 Honeycrisp or other tart apples, unpeeled, cored, and cut into 8 wedges
1 large or 2 medium leeks (white and light green parts only), sliced into ½-inch (1 cm) thick rounds
2 tablespoons (30 mL) bacon fat or olive oil
1 teaspoon (5 mL) sea salt
Freshly ground black pepper
1 lemon, halved
10 ounces (280 g) fresh arugula

DRY BRINING
Seasoning Method

Lightly salting meat and giving the seasoning time to penetrate. Salt initially draws moisture to the meat's surface, but given time the meat eventually reabsorbs the liquid along with the seasoning. The effect is even seasoning throughout the meat.

COFFEE SPICE–RUBBED PORK TENDERLOIN

Juicy pork tenderloin slowly grilled with an intriguingly smoky spice rub until a delicious crust forms. Caramelized grilled pineapple, sweet red onion, and just spicy enough poblano, tossed with cooling cilantro and dressed with bright lime.

COFFEE SPICE–RUB THE PORK

In a small bowl, whisk together the ground espresso, brown sugar, coarse salt, black pepper, garlic powder, onion powder, paprika, cumin, and cayenne pepper. Pat dry the pork tenderloins with paper towel. Evenly season each tenderloin with 2 tablespoons (30 mL) or so of the rub. Let rest at room temperature as the seasoning finds its way into the meat, an hour or so. Transfer the remaining rub to a mason jar, seal tightly, and store in a cool, dark place for up to 6 months.

BUILD A FIRE

Build and tend an active fire in your firepit, bringing to medium-high heat with live flame and a growing bed of glowing hot coals. Position a lightly oiled grill grate directly over the fire. Alternatively, light your charcoal grill or fire up your gas grill to its highest setting.

MEANWHILE, MAKE THE GRILLED PINEAPPLE, POBLANO, RED ONION, AND CILANTRO SALAD

In a large bowl, whisk together the lime zest and juice, honey, and ¼ cup (60 mL) of the olive oil. Reserve.

Pour the remaining 2 tablespoons (30 mL) olive oil onto a rimmed baking sheet. Spread the pineapple slices around the pan, sliding and turning until evenly coated in oil. Lightly season both sides with sea salt. Stack the pineapple in one corner of the pan. Repeat with the poblanos and red onions, adding more olive oil and salt as needed, taking care not to disturb the nested onion rings.

When the fire is hottest, transfer the pineapple, poblanos, and onion slices to the grill and sear, turning occasionally, until the pineapple is charred, caramelized, and tender and the poblanos and onions are lightly charred and softened. Transfer the onions to the lime dressing. Transfer the pineapple and poblanos to a cutting board. Cut each pineapple slice into 8 wedges and finely chop the poblanos. Add to the onions with every last drop of juice from the cutting board. Toss together and reserve.

GRILL THE PORK TENDERLOIN

As the fire dies down, grill the pork, turning occasionally, allowing the full flavours of the spice rub to shine without being scorched, 15 minutes or so. The pork is done when an instant-read thermometer in the thickest part of the meat registers 145°F (63°C). Transfer to a resting platter, cover loosely with foil, and let rest for 10 minutes before slicing.

Add the cilantro to the pineapple mixture and toss once more. Thinly slice the pork and serve with the grilled pineapple, poblano, red onion, and cilantro salad.

SERVES 4 TO 6, WITH LEFTOVER COFFEE SPICE RUB

SPECIAL EQUIPMENT NEEDED: digital instant-read thermometer

COFFEE SPICE–RUBBED PORK TENDERLOIN (MAKES ABOUT 2 CUPS/500 ML OF RUB)

½ cup (125 mL) ground espresso beans

½ cup (125 mL) firmly packed brown sugar

½ cup (125 mL) coarse salt

2 tablespoons (30 mL) freshly ground black pepper

2 tablespoons (30 mL) garlic powder

2 tablespoons (30 mL) onion powder

2 tablespoons (30 mL) smoked paprika

2 tablespoons (30 mL) ground cumin

1 teaspoon (5 mL) cayenne pepper

2 pork tenderloins (1 pound/450 g each), silverskins trimmed, cut in half lengthwise

GRILLED PINEAPPLE, POBLANO, RED ONION, AND CILANTRO SALAD

Zest and juice of 2 limes

1 tablespoon (15 mL) pure liquid honey

¼ cup (60 mL) + 2 tablespoons (30 mL) olive oil, divided, more as needed

½ teaspoon (2 mL) sea salt, plus more for sprinkling

1 ripe pineapple, peeled, core left intact, cut into 1-inch (2.5 cm) thick slices

2 poblano peppers, halved, stem, seeds, and pith discarded

2 large red onions, peeled, cut into ½-inch (1 cm) thick slices

Whole leaves and minced tender stems from 1 bunch of fresh cilantro

COFFEE RUB
Fire Kitchen Ingredient

An aromatic spice rub blended with ground coffee for its heavenly complementary and subtly smoky flavour base. Best used to season slowly cooked or smoked meats to protect the flavours from damaging heat while allowing an exquisite crust to form.

BUTTERMILK-BRINED PORK CHOPS
WITH CHARRED CORN AND GREEN ONION SALSA

Thick pork chops patiently brined and tenderized with tangy buttermilk before being grilled. The perfect accompaniment must be this mouth-watering charred corn tossed with grilled poblano pepper and herbaceous green onion in a tangy salsa brightened with lightly toasted whole spices along with traditional cilantro.

BRINE THE PORK CHOPS

In a large bowl, whisk together the buttermilk, garlic, salt, paprika, and cayenne pepper. Arrange the pork chops in a single layer in a large baking pan that fits them snugly. Pour the brine over them. Cover tightly and refrigerate overnight.

BUILD A FIRE

Build and tend an active fire in your firepit, bringing to medium-high heat with live flame and a growing bed of glowing hot coals. Position a lightly oiled grill grate directly over the fire. Alternatively, light your charcoal grill or fire up your gas grill to its highest setting.

MAKE THE CHARRED CORN AND GREEN ONION SALSA

Lightly coat the corn, bell pepper, and poblano pepper with the olive oil. Grill the vegetables over the hottest fire, turning frequently, until tender and lightly charred, 10 minutes or so. Transfer the vegetables to a resting platter until cool enough to handle. In a large bowl, holding each cob of corn upright, with a sharp knife shave the kernels away from the cob into the bowl. Finely chop the peppers and add to the corn.

In a small dry skillet over medium heat, gently warm the cumin seeds, coriander seeds, and fennel seeds until fragrant and lightly toasted, just 2 or 3 minutes. Add the seeds, green onions, cilantro, lime zest and juice, and salt to the corn mixture. Lightly toss to combine.

GRILL THE PORK CHOPS

Remove the pork chops from the brine and drain well. As the fire dies down, grill the pork, turning occasionally, until browned and tender. The pork is done when an instant-read thermometer in the thickest part of the meat registers 145°F (63°C). Serve immediately with a hearty spoonful of corn salsa.

SERVES 4 TO 6

SPECIAL EQUIPMENT NEEDED: digital instant-read thermometer

BUTTERMILK-BRINED PORK CHOPS

4 cups (1 L) buttermilk

4 garlic cloves, finely grated with a microplane or finely minced

2 tablespoons (30 mL) sea salt

2 tablespoons (30 mL) smoked paprika, chili powder, or Old Bay seasoning

1 teaspoon (5 mL) cayenne pepper

4 to 6 (1-inch/2.5 cm thick) bone-in pork loin chops (about 12 ounces/340 g each)

CHARRED CORN AND GREEN ONION SALSA

4 sweet corncobs, shucked

1 red bell pepper, quartered, stem, seeds, and pith discarded

1 poblano pepper, quartered, stem, seeds, and pith discarded

2 tablespoons (30 mL) olive oil

1 tablespoon (15 mL) cumin seeds

1 tablespoon (15 mL) coriander seeds

1 tablespoon (15 mL) fennel seeds

4 green onions, thinly sliced

Leaves and tender stems from 1 bunch of fresh cilantro, minced

Zest and juice of 2 juicy limes

1 teaspoon (5 mL) sea salt

BUTTERMILK BRINING
Cooking Method

Pork and chicken can be very lean and thus dry out quickly over a fierce fire. Brining helps them retain moisture and adds flavour. Buttermilk goes further by tenderizing the meat.

VIETNAMESE PORK CHOPS WITH FRESH HERB AND BEAN SPROUT SALAD

Brightly marinated and pleasantly charred tender, juicy pork chops paired with aromatic fresh herbs, crunchy bean sprouts, and enough sweet, spicy juices to dress into an authentically delicious salad.

FLATTEN AND MARINATE THE PORK CHOPS

Position a sheet of plastic wrap on a work surface. Lightly spray with oil. Place a pork chop in the centre of the plastic. Cover with a second sheet of plastic wrap. Vigorously pound the pork with the bottom of a small pan, flattening and increasing the surface area until about ½ inch (1 cm) thick. Carefully transfer the pork chop to a large resealable freezer bag. Repeat with the remaining chops.

In a small bowl, stir together the shallots, garlic, brown sugar, fish sauce, soy sauce, and vegetable oil until thoroughly mixed and the sugar is dissolved. Transfer to the pork chop bag and seal. Carefully massage the marinade into the meat. Squeeze out most of the air and tightly seal the bag. Lay flat in a baking pan to contain any inadvertent mess. Refrigerate for at least 4 hours or, for best results, overnight, turning once or twice.

BUILD A FIRE

Build and tend an active fire in your firepit, bringing to medium-high heat with live flame and a growing bed of glowing hot coals. Position a lightly oiled grill grate directly over the fire. Alternatively, light your charcoal grill or fire up your gas grill to its highest setting.

GRILL THE PORK CHOPS

Remove the pork chops from the marinade and drain well. Grill, turning once, until browned, lightly charred, and rosy-pink tender. The pork is done when an instant-read thermometer in the thickest part of the meat registers 145°F (63°C). Transfer to a platter and let rest to the side of the fire before slicing.

MAKE THE FRESH HERB AND BEAN SPROUT SALAD

In a large bowl, toss together the cinnamon basil, cilantro, mint, green onions, bean sprouts, chili, and sriracha pickled red onions and their juice.

Serve the pork chops on individual plates topped with a tangled handful of salad. Or to serve communally, thinly slice the chops and toss with the herb salad and all the accumulated juices. Serve with lime wedges.

SERVES 4 TO 6

SPECIAL EQUIPMENT NEEDED: digital instant-read thermometer

4 (1-inch/2.5 cm thick) bone-in pork loin chops (about 12 ounces/340 g each)

VIETNAMESE MARINADE

2 large shallots, minced

4 garlic cloves, grated with a microplane into a paste

½ cup (125 mL) firmly packed brown sugar

½ cup (125 mL) fish sauce

¼ cup (60 mL) soy sauce

2 tablespoons (30 mL) vegetable oil

FRESH HERB AND BEAN SPROUT SALAD

Leaves and tender stems from a handful of fresh cinnamon basil or Thai basil

Leaves and tender stems from a handful of fresh cilantro

Leaves and tender stems from a handful of fresh mint

2 green onions, very thinly sliced

2 cups (500 mL) fresh bean sprouts

A fresh medium-heat chili, stem, seeds, and pith discarded, very thinly sliced

¼ cup (60 mL) Sriracha Pickled Red Onions (page 258) + 2 tablespoons (30 mL) pickling juice

2 limes, cut into wedges

FLATTENING MEAT
Fire Kitchen Technique

An ancient method for tenderizing tougher meat cuts and flavouring tender cuts. Increased surface area increases tenderness and juiciness through rapid cooking. High searing heat allows for deliciously charred exterior flavour development without extended cooking times that would dry out the meat.

CUBAN MOJO CHICKEN AND CHARRED PEPPERS WITH CUBAN SOUR ORANGE SAUCE

Cuba's classic citrus-based mojo is an all-purpose sauce traditionally used as a marinade, for basting during cooking, and as a finishing sauce. When authentic sour oranges aren't available, their distinctive flavours are easily approximated with orange and lime. Sweet peppers are appetizingly self-smoking—as they grill, they absorb the smoky flavours of their charring skin.

MAKE THE MOJO SAUCE AND MARINATE THE CHICKEN

In a high-speed blender, combine the orange zest and juice, garlic, jalapeños, olive oil, honey, oregano, cumin, and salt. Purée until smooth.

Place the chicken thighs in a medium metal bowl and cover with the marinade, stirring to coat evenly. Cover tightly and refrigerate overnight.

BUILD A FIRE

Build and tend an active fire in your firepit, bringing to medium-high heat with live flame and a growing bed of glowing hot coals. Position a lightly oiled grill grate directly over the fire. Alternatively, light your charcoal grill or fire up your gas grill to its highest setting.

CHAR THE PEPPERS AND CITRUS

In a large bowl, toss the pepper pieces with the vegetable oil and lightly season with salt. Place the orange and lime halves cut side down on the grate and the peppers skin side down. Grill, leaving the citrus undisturbed but turning the peppers occasionally, until charred and softened, 10 minutes or so. With a pair of tongs, thoroughly squeeze the citrus juices through a strainer into a medium bowl. Transfer the peppers to a cutting board. Thinly slice the peppers, transfer them to the bowl, and toss together with the citrus juices.

GRILL THE CHICKEN AND REHEAT THE SAUCE

Remove the chicken thighs from the marinade. Transfer the marinade to a small saucepan and bring to a full simmer, stirring constantly. Add the marinade to the sliced peppers. Let rest near the fire.

Grill the chicken thighs, turning frequently, until tender, golden brown, and lightly charred, 10 minutes or so. The chicken is done when an instant-read thermometer in the thickest part of the meat registers at least 165°F (74°C). Transfer the chicken to the bowl of sliced peppers and let rest a few minutes. Thinly slice the chicken and return to the bowl. Add the cilantro and toss together with any accumulated juices. Serve immediately.

SERVES 4 TO 6

SPECIAL EQUIPMENT NEEDED: digital instant-read thermometer

CUBAN MOJO CHICKEN

Zest and juice of 2 Cuban sour oranges (or the zest and juice of 1 large fragrant orange and 4 large juicy limes)

Cloves from 1 head of garlic, peeled and roughly chopped

2 jalapeño peppers

1 cup (250 mL) olive oil

1 tablespoon (15 mL) pure liquid honey

1 tablespoon (15 mL) dried oregano

1 tablespoon (15 mL) ground cumin

1 tablespoon (15 mL) salt

12 skinless, boneless chicken thighs (about 3 pounds/1.35 kg total)

CHARRED PEPPERS AND CITRUS

1 poblano pepper, halved, stem, seeds, and pith discarded, flattened

1 green bell pepper, halved, stem, seeds, and pith discarded, flattened

1 red bell pepper, halved, stem, seeds, and pith discarded, flattened

1 orange bell pepper, halved, stem, seeds, and pith discarded, flattened

1 yellow bell pepper, halved, stem, seeds, and pith discarded, flattened

2 tablespoons (30 mL) vegetable oil

Sea salt

2 oranges, halved

2 limes, halved

Leaves and tender stems from 1 bunch of fresh cilantro, lightly chopped

ACIDIC MARINADE
Fire Kitchen Method

A vinegar- or citrus juice–based marinade that tenderizes meat by weakening its protein and collagen bonds, adds juiciness as the broken proteins trap juicy water molecules as they re-form, and creates characteristic flavour with aromatic ingredients.

SPICED YOGURT MARINATED CHICKEN THIGH SKEWERS WITH GRILLED FENNEL, CHARRED TOMATO, AND FRESH BASIL SALAD

Versatile chicken thighs patiently marinated and then grilled over the fire for the juiciest flavour. Fiercely charred tomatoes mashed into a lemony dressing for a warm salad of aromatic fresh basil leaves and sweet fennel softened and caramelized by the fire.

MARINATE THE CHICKEN

To a food processor, add the yogurt, lemon zest and juice, onion, garlic, tomato paste, paprika, fennel seeds, cumin, salt, and chili flakes. Process until smooth. Transfer to a large bowl. Add the chicken and toss with the marinade until thoroughly coated. Cover tightly and refrigerate overnight.

BUILD A FIRE

Build and tend an active fire in your firepit, bringing to medium-high heat with live flame and a growing bed of glowing hot coals. Position a lightly oiled grill grate directly over the fire and have ready fitted crossbars for suspending the skewers without the grill. Alternatively, light your charcoal grill or fire up your gas grill to its highest setting.

GRILL THE FENNEL AND TOMATOES

In a large bowl toss the fennel with the olive oil and salt. Grill the fennel over medium-high heat, turning occasionally, until softened and lightly charred, 10 minutes or so. Meanwhile, grill the tomatoes cut side down over the fiercest heat of the fire, without disturbing, turning once, until charred, softened, and fully cooked, 5 minutes or so. Transfer the tomatoes to the large bowl. Add the preserved lemon purée and mash with a potato masher into a coarse sauce. Add the fennel and lightly toss, coating with the sauce. Just before serving, add the basil leaves.

ROAST THE CHICKEN

Remove the chicken thighs from the marinade, allowing some to cling to the meat. Tightly thread 2 or 3 thighs onto a pair of skewers. Tend the fire down to a glowing bed of active embers, lowering its heat. Remove the grate and re-rig for skewers. Suspend the skewers above the open fire and roast, turning occasionally, until browned and tender. The chicken is safely done when an instant-read thermometer in the thickest part of the meat registers 165°F (74°C), but it's even more flavourful when it lingers in the sweet spot of the fire, slowly rising as high as 190°F (88°C) before it begins drying out. Transfer to a resting plate.

Serve individually or communally. Slide the chicken off the skewers and serve over a heaping spoonful of grilled fennel, charred tomato, and fresh basil salad. Garnish with reserved basil sprigs.

SERVES 4 TO 6

SPECIAL EQUIPMENT NEEDED:
12 bamboo skewers, soaked in water overnight, or metal skewers; digital instant-read thermometer

SPICED YOGURT MARINATED CHICKEN THIGHS

1 cup (250 mL) natural plain full-fat yogurt or plain Greek yogurt

Zest and juice of 1 lemon

1 small yellow or white onion, chopped

4 garlic cloves, chopped

2 tablespoons (30 mL) tomato paste

2 tablespoons (30 mL) smoked paprika

2 tablespoons (30 mL) fennel seeds

1 tablespoon (15 mL) ground cumin

2 teaspoons (20 mL) sea salt

1 teaspoon (5 mL) red chili flakes

8 skinless, bone-in chicken thighs (about 2 pounds/900 g total)

GRILLED FENNEL, CHARRED TOMATO, AND FRESH BASIL SALAD

2 fennel bulbs, trimmed, cores intact, each cut into 4 wedges

2 tablespoons (30 mL) olive oil

½ teaspoon (2 mL) sea salt

4 ripe plum tomatoes, halved through core

1 tablespoon (15 mL) Preserved Lemon Purée (page 257)

Leaves from 1 bunch of fresh basil, a few sprigs reserved for garnish

YOGURT MARINADE
Fire Kitchen Method

An all-purpose marinade utilizing the distinctive properties of yogurt to tenderize leaner meats, adding rich juiciness, tangy flavour, and aromatic character. Yogurt marinades are notoriously sticky, though, so meats are often suspended over the fire rather than allowed direct damaging contact with metal grills.

GRILLED CHICKEN THIGH SALAD

Chicken thighs are perfect for grilling. They're economical, juicy, simple to sear and brown, and easily absorb the caramelized flavours of high-heat cooking. In this bright summer salad, the classic grilling marinade does double duty as an equally delicious dressing for the finished salad.

SERVES 4 TO 6

SPECIAL EQUIPMENT NEEDED: digital instant-read thermometer

LEMON MUSTARD MARINADE DRESSING

½ cup (125 mL) extra-virgin olive oil

Zest and juice of 1 lemon

2 garlic cloves, finely grated with a microplane

2 tablespoons (30 mL) Dijon mustard

1 tablespoon (15 mL) Preserved Lemon Purée (page 257)

1 tablespoon (15 mL) pure liquid honey

1 teaspoon (5 mL) sea salt

GRILLED CHICKEN THIGH SALAD

8 skinless, boneless chicken thighs (about 2 pounds/900 g total)

1 large English-style cucumber

½ teaspoon (2 mL) sea salt

½ teaspoon (2 mL) sugar

2 jalapeño peppers

1 can (19 ounces/540 mL) chickpeas, drained and rinsed

1 red onion, thinly sliced

Leaves and tender stems from 1 bunch of fresh mint

MARINADE DRESSING
Fire Kitchen Ingredient

An all-purpose sauce, perfect for a long-flavoured soak, a bright last-minute salad dressing, and a last-second condiment. Bright, acidic marinades and dressings share many similarities and are thus often used interchangeably.

MAKE THE LEMON MUSTARD MARINADE DRESSING

In a large bowl, whisk together the olive oil, lemon zest and juice, garlic, mustard, preserved lemon purée, honey, and salt until smooth. Pour half the dressing into a small jar and reserve.

MARINATE THE CHICKEN

Add the chicken thighs to the remaining dressing. Toss until fully and evenly coated with the marinade. Cover tightly and refrigerate for at least an hour or two or overnight.

SMASH THE CUCUMBERS

Cut the cucumber in half lengthwise, then crosswise. Lay the cucumber pieces cut side down on your work surface. One at a time, cover each cucumber length with the blade of a large knife. Firmly press down, smashing, even smacking, until the skin cracks, the flesh breaks, and the seeds release. Slice diagonally into bite-size pieces. Discard the seeds. In a medium bowl toss the cucumber pieces with the salt and sugar. Transfer to a strainer set in a bowl, refrigerate, and let drain until chilled and crisp, an hour or so.

BUILD A FIRE

Build and tend an active fire in your firepit, bringing to medium-high heat with live flame and a growing bed of glowing hot coals. Position a lightly oiled grill grate directly over the fire. Alternatively, light your charcoal grill or fire up your gas grill to its highest setting.

GRILL THE CHICKEN AND ASSEMBLE THE SALAD

Remove the chicken thighs from the marinade. Place the chicken on the grate and grill, turning occasionally, until browned, tender, and cooked through. Grill the jalapeños to one side, turning occasionally, until charred and softened, then transfer to a resting platter and let rest until cool. The chicken is safely done when an instant-read thermometer in the thickest part of the meat registers 165°F (74°C), but it's even tastier when it lingers in the sweet spot of the fire, slowly rising as high as 190°F (88°C) before it begins drying out. Transfer to the platter with the jalapeños and let rest for 5 minutes before slicing.

Slice the rested chicken thighs into bite-size pieces. Transfer to a serving bowl. Cut the jalapeños in half and discard the stems, seeds, and pith. Mince the jalapeño and add to the chicken along with the cucumber, chickpeas, red onion, mint (if serving immediately) and reserved lemon mustard marinade dressing. Serve immediately. Alternatively, let rest for an hour or so, going with the flow of the party while allowing the salad's flavours and textures to mingle further, then toss with the mint just before serving.

WOOD-ROASTED SPATCHCOCK CHICKEN, BABY POTATOES, AND LEEKS WITH ROASTED LEMON GARLIC DRESSING

SERVES 4 TO 6

The incomparable flavours of wood oven roasting are perhaps best enjoyed in a simple roast chicken. A spatchcocked chicken, flattened for easier cooking, roasted over hearty potatoes and tender leeks, finished with an easy pan dressing of roasted lemon and mellow garlic.

SPATCHCOCK THE CHICKEN

Position the chicken breast side down on a baking sheet to help contain the mess. Using poultry shears, cut firmly along each side of the backbone. Remove and reserve for broth. Flip the chicken over and open onto the baking sheet. Grasp the legs and thighs and bend them back. With your hands, press firmly on the breasts to flatten the chicken—you'll feel the breastbone crack. Generously season both sides with salt and pepper.

BUILD A FIRE

Build and tend an active fire in your wood oven, bringing to medium roasting temperature and a bed of glowing hot coals. Push coals to the back, clearing a roasting area to the front. Monitor the cooking temperature with a high-temperature ovenproof thermometer or infrared thermometer. Tend the fire, bringing the oven to 400°F (200°C) or so. Alternatively, preheat your indoor oven.

PREP THE ROAST

Fill a 16-inch (40 cm) cast-iron skillet or heavy roasting pan with the potatoes and leeks. Cover with the seasoned chicken, skin side up. Nestle the garlic and lemons cut side up around the chicken.

ROAST THE CHICKEN

Place the chicken in the wood oven and roast, shaking, settling, and rotating the pan frequently, moving it closer to or farther from the fire, until the chicken skin is golden brown, even lightly charred. Turn the chicken over, shake and settle the pan, and continue roasting until the potatoes are tender and the underside of the chicken is browned, 30 minutes or so total. The chicken is done when an instant-read thermometer in the thickest part of the breast meat and thigh registers at least 165°F (74°C). Turn over once again and roast a few minutes longer to recrisp the skin. Remove from the oven.

With two pairs of tongs, pull and shred every morsel of tender meat and crispy skin from the chicken carcass directly into the pan. Carefully remove the leg and thigh bones and reserve with the carcass and backbone for broth. With a pair of tongs, squeeze each of the juicy lemons and roasted garlic heads directly into the pan. Sprinkle with parsley. Gently stir together the flavours until evenly combined. Serve immediately with an array of sides and salads.

SPECIAL EQUIPMENT NEEDED: wood oven; 16-inch (40 cm) cast-iron skillet or heavy roasting pan; high-temperature ovenproof thermometer, infrared thermometer, or digital instant-read thermometer

1 large roasting chicken (about 4 pounds/ 1.8 kg)

Sea salt

Freshly ground black pepper

2 pounds (900 g) baby potatoes

2 leeks (white and light green parts only), sliced into 1-inch (2.5 cm) thick rounds

2 heads of garlic, top inch (2.5 cm) trimmed

2 lemons, halved

A handful of fresh parsley sprigs, finely chopped

SPATCHCOCKING CHICKEN
Fire Kitchen Method

Removing the backbone of a chicken so the bird can be flattened for grilling or roasting. This butcher's method, also known as butterflying, makes the chicken easier to handle, maximizes delicious surface area, adds deeper flavour, and allows for more even and quicker cooking.

GRILLED CHICKEN WINGS WITH FOUR SPICY SAUCES

Chicken wings are ideal for grilling, easily becoming addictively crispy and caramelized. The secret is low and slow heat that cooks without burning, glowing coals creating smoky flavours as juices drip onto them. Easily cooked wings, delicious as is or ready for dressing up with your favourite wing sauce.

BUILD A FIRE

Build and tend a slow fire in your firepit, bringing to medium-low to low heat with no live flame and a thick bed of glowing coals. Position a lightly oiled grill grate directly over the fire. Alternatively, light your charcoal grill or fire up your gas grill to its medium-low setting.

GRILL THE CHICKEN WINGS

In a large bowl, toss the wings with the vegetable oil and salt until evenly coated. Position the wings over the fire and slowly grill, turning occasionally, moving as needed if the skin begins to brown too quickly or to avoid flare-ups, continuing until cooked through, crispy, golden brown, even lightly charred, 30 to 40 minutes.

SAUCE THE WINGS

Transfer the grilled wings to a large bowl and toss with your favourite sauce. Serve immediately.

SERVES 4 TO 6

GRILLED CHICKEN WINGS
5 pounds (2.25 kg) whole chicken wings
2 tablespoons (30 mL) vegetable oil
1 tablespoon (15 mL) kosher salt

SAUCE OPTIONS (PICK YOUR FAVOURITE)
Classic Buffalo Sauce (page 259)
Ancho Barbecue Sauce (page 260)
Chipotle Barbecue Sauce (page 261)
Gochujang Ginger Sauce (page 261)

GRILLING CHICKEN WINGS
Fire Cooking Method

A low-heat cooking method that yields the perfect ratio of crispy skin, caramelized flavour, and tender, juicy meat. Grilled wings are best sauced after cooking with a brightly flavoured condiment to emphasize the roast chicken flavours rather than dulling the sauce through glazing, charring, and burning. Whole chicken wings are much easier to handle on the grill.

MINTED LAMB KOFTA WITH SUMAC LABNEH

Lamb koftas are found throughout the Middle East, and years ago they came to Prince Edward Island with our many Lebanese neighbours. Today they are a menu regular in our Fire Garden. Labneh is a tasty, rich drained yogurt thickened into a flavour-packed cheese-like condiment infused here with bright red tangy sumac from our farm.

MAKE THE SUMAC LABNEH

In a small bowl, whisk together the yogurt, preserved lemon purée, and sumac. Transfer the mixture to a strainer lined with folded cheesecloth and suspended over a bowl. Cover completely with plastic wrap and let drain in the refrigerator for 24 hours. Discard the whey. Use immediately or transfer to a resealable container and refrigerate for up to 3 days.

PREP THE KOFTAS

In a large bowl, combine the lamb, mint, onion, garlic, molasses, paprika, cumin, chili flakes, and salt. Mix well with your hands until evenly combined. Divide and shape the mixture into 12 sausages, 1 inch (2.5 cm) thick. Thread onto the skewers. Cover tightly and refrigerate until thoroughly chilled, an hour or so.

BUILD A FIRE

Build and tend an active fire in your firepit, bringing to medium-high heat with live flame and a growing bed of glowing hot coals. Position skewer supports as needed directly over the fire. Alternatively, light your charcoal grill or fire up your gas grill to its highest setting.

SEAR THE KOFTA KABOBS

Season the lamb skewers lightly with salt. Position the skewers above the open fire and roast, turning occasionally, until browned yet still slightly pink in the centre, 8 to 10 minutes. Transfer to a resting platter.

Serve the minted lamb kofta skewers with the sumac labneh, lettuce leaves, lemon wedges, and mint sprigs. Let guests assemble their own. Wrap each kofta in a lettuce leaf, hold firmly, remove the skewer, smear with labneh, garnish with a mint sprig, and sprinkle with freshly squeezed lemon juice.

SERVES 4 TO 6, WITH LEFTOVER SUMAC LABNEH

SPECIAL EQUIPMENT NEEDED: 12 metal skewers

SUMAC LABNEH

2 cups (500 mL) natural plain full-fat yogurt or plain Greek yogurt

2 tablespoons (30 mL) Preserved Lemon Purée (page 257)

1 tablespoon (15 mL) ground sumac

MINTED LAMB KOFTA

2 pounds (900 g) ground lamb

Leaves and tender stems from 1 bunch of fresh mint, finely chopped, a few sprigs reserved for garnish

1 small yellow or white onion, finely grated with a microplane

4 garlic cloves, finely grated with a microplane

2 tablespoons (30 mL) pomegranate molasses or pure liquid honey

2 tablespoons (30 mL) smoked paprika

1 tablespoon (15 mL) ground cumin

1 tablespoon (15 mL) red chili flakes

1 tablespoon (15 mL) sea salt, plus more for seasoning

FOR SERVING

2 heads of Bibb lettuce, leaves separated

2 lemons, cut into wedges

METAL SKEWERS
Fire Kitchen Tool

An essential tool in the fire kitchens of the world for suspending food directly over a fire. Many ingredients require high searing heat but don't fare well in direct contact with a grill, no matter how hot the metal of the grate.

STRING-ROASTED LEG OF LAMB WITH MINT CHIMICHURRI

A slowly spinning leg of lamb, connected to the ages, basting in radiant heat and aromatic wood smoke, deliciously roasting. An equally classic condiment brightened with familiar fragrant mint.

PREP THE LAMB LEG

Generously rub the entire surface of the lamb leg with the old-school dry rub. Rest the roast on a baking sheet. Cover with plastic wrap. Let rest at room temperature as the seasoning finds its way into the meat, at least 1 hour but no more than 2.

BUILD A FIRE

Build and tend an active fire in your firepit, bringing to medium-high heat with a growing bed of glowing hot coals.

STRING-ROAST THE LAMB

With a sharp knife tip, pierce the narrow end of the lamb leg, between the tendon and the bone. Thread the string through the hole. Tie the ends of the string together, forming a loop. Hang from the suspension point well above the fire. Position the lamb just above and to the side of the fire in the direct radiant heat zone. Gently spin the leg, winding up the string. Release it, allowing it to slowly unwind until it spins in the other direction, then back again, eventually returning to its slow finish. Sit back and easily tend the lamb by occasionally tapping it gently on the side with the stick with just enough force and rhythm to keep it spinning gently. Slowly roast the lamb leg for a full hour or more, searing and developing the flavourful crust, tending the fire slowly down, continuing until an instant-read thermometer in the thickest part of the roast registers 135°F (57°C). Let rest in a warm place, away from the direct heat, for 20 minutes before slicing.

Thinly slice the lamb. Towards the thicker end you'll find rosy, pink slices for the medium-rare crowd, while the well-done fans will prefer the thinner end. Serve with lots of mint chimichurri and an array of sides and salads.

SERVES 8

SPECIAL EQUIPMENT NEEDED: 8- to 12-foot (2.5 to 3.5 m) length of heavy-duty cotton butcher's string, soaked in water; cooking tripod or adjustable suspension point 6 inches (15 cm) above the fire; hardwood stick about 1 foot (30 cm) thick and 4 feet (1.2 m) long, trimmed, one end whittled and sharpened; digital instant-read thermometer

1 bone-in leg of lamb, aitch bone removed (about 6 pounds/2.7 kg)
¼ cup (60 mL) Old-School Dry Rub (page 256)
1 batch Mint Chimichurri (page 259)

STRING ROASTING
Bushcraft Cooking Method

A vertical rotisserie-like technique harnessing the steady back-and-forth inertia of a slowly rotating weight on a spinning string. A historical method developed independently by cooks around the world to patiently roast meat without burning it.

DESERT-STYLE LAMB TAGINE WITH COUSCOUS

A tagine is both a North African cooking vessel with a distinctive conical lid and the name given to the traditional stews prepared within. A tagine stew is sweet and savoury, deeply perfumed with a blend of spices and prepared simply with common ingredients from the region. It often includes chickpeas, dried or preserved fruits, dried nuts, lamb, sheep, or goat. The tagine is also a fascinating example of what a culture can do with precious little wood.

BUILD A FIRE

Build and tend a small fire in your firepit. Position a grill grate directly over the fire. Preheat the base of a 12-inch (30 cm) traditional tagine or a large cast-iron Dutch oven over the flames to capture the initial heat of the fire before the glowing coals ahead.

MAKE THE LAMB TAGINE

Melt the butter in the tagine. Stir in the grated onion, garlic, tomato paste, cinnamon, cumin, cardamom, coriander, ginger, chili flakes, harissa paste, apricot preserves, and red wine vinegar. Continue stirring just long enough for the mixture to simmer, then add the olives, dates, and lamb. Stir slowly as the spices and flavours begin permeating the lamb, continuing without browning until the meat is heated through, 5 minutes or so.

Stir in the chickpeas and salt. Carefully reposition over very low heat. Slowly pour in the orange juice, completely filling the base of the tagine with as much flavourful moisture as possible but trying to leave the narrow rim dry. Top with the lid. Fill the top cup with cooling water, encouraging the steam within to condense and drip back into the simmering stew. Simmer over very low heat, carefully moving the vessel as the flames die down to rest directly in the embers, continuing until the lamb is very tender, an hour or so. Keep an eye on the raised lip where the top fits the bottom: moisture flowing down the sloped sides creates a bubbling air lock that experienced cooks use to gauge the hidden progress within. Gentle bubbling shows that the stew is simmering slowly. After an hour remove from the heat and let rest for 30 minutes or so before serving. Stir in the mint and lemon zest and juice at the last second.

MAKE THE COUSCOUS

While the tagine cooks, in a medium saucepan bring the broth, olive oil, and salt to a full boil. Stir in the couscous, cover tightly, and remove from the heat. Let rest as the grains absorb the steamy moisture, swelling and tenderizing, 5 minutes or more. Just before serving, fluff with a fork, breaking into flavourful clumps.

Divide the couscous between bowls. Ladle the tagine over the couscous. Sprinkle with the almonds and reserved herb sprigs.

SERVES 4 TO 6

SPECIAL EQUIPMENT NEEDED: 12-inch (30 cm) tagine or large cast-iron Dutch oven

LAMB TAGINE

2 tablespoons (30 mL) butter or olive oil

1 large yellow onion, grated on the large holes of a box grater

4 garlic cloves, minced

¼ cup (60 mL) tomato paste

1 teaspoon (5 mL) cinnamon

1 teaspoon (5 mL) ground cumin

1 teaspoon (5 mL) ground cardamom

1 teaspoon (5 mL) ground coriander

1 teaspoon (5 mL) ground ginger

¼ teaspoon (1 mL) red chili flakes

1 teaspoon (5 mL) harissa paste

½ cup (125 mL) apricot preserves

¼ cup (60 mL) red wine vinegar

½ cup (125 mL) chopped pitted Kalamata olives

½ cup (125 mL) chopped pitted Medjool dates or raisins

2 pounds (900 g) lamb shoulder, leg, or stew meat, cut into 1½-inch (4 cm) pieces

1 can (14 ounces/398 mL) chickpeas, drained and rinsed

1 teaspoon (5 mL) sea salt

2 cups (500 mL) orange juice, chicken, lamb, or vegetable broth, or water

½ cup (125 mL) chopped fresh mint, cilantro, or curly or flat-leaf parsley, a few sprigs reserved for garnish

Zest and juice of 1 lemon

½ cup (125 mL) slivered almonds

COUSCOUS

1½ cups (375 mL) chicken, lamb, or vegetable broth or water

2 tablespoons (30 mL) extra-virgin olive oil

1 teaspoon (5 mL) sea salt

1½ cups (375 mL) couscous

DESERT STYLE
Traditional Cooking Methods

A style of cooking necessitated by the scarcity and challenges of the desert. The cooking vessel's design preserves scarce moisture. The distinctive conical top and its characteristic cooling cup encourage the precious fragrant liquid within to recondense above the stew and slowly roll back down the sides into the works.

WOOD-FIRED SEAFOOD

IRON-STEAMED MUSSELS WITH TOMATO BASIL BROTH AND FIRE TOAST

Easily cooked tasty fresh mussels and their delightfully briny broth made fragrant with tomato, garlic, and fresh basil. Hearty bread, lightly scorched, infused with raw garlic, then topped with rich, briny butter with even more garlic, this time smooth, mellow roasted garlic.

BUILD A FIRE

Build and tend an active fire in your firepit, bringing to medium-high heat with some live flame and a growing bed of glowing hot coals. Position a grill grate directly over the fire. Alternatively, light your charcoal grill or fire up your gas grill to its highest setting. Warm a large cast-iron Dutch oven on the grate or next to the fire.

ROAST THE GARLIC FOR THE ANCHOVY BUTTER

Position the garlic heads to the side of the main fire or in a cooler spot on the grill and slowly roast, turning occasionally, until softened, charred, and juices begin to ooze from the top, 20 to 30 minutes. Let rest away from the fire until cool enough to handle.

MEANWHILE, MAKE THE TOMATO BASIL BROTH

Splash the olive oil into the hot Dutch oven. Add the onion and carrots and cook, stirring constantly, until softened and fragrant but not browned, 2 or 3 minutes. Add the garlic, chili flakes, and salt and continue stirring until fragrant but not browned, just a minute or so. Pour in the wine and simmer just long enough for it to reduce by half. Stir in the tomatoes and bring to a slow, steady simmer. The broth is ready. Move to the side of the fire until needed.

FINISH THE ROASTED GARLIC BUTTER

When the roasted garlic is cool, use a serrated knife to slice off the tops. Squeeze the soft cloves into a small bowl. Add the butter, anchovies, lemon zest and juice, and parsley and stir together until well combined. Reserve.

STEAM THE MUSSELS

Add the mussels to the broth. Carefully position the Dutch oven on the grill, over the direct fire. Cover tightly and steam, cooking the mussels until they open and release their rich, fragrant broth, 10 minutes or so. Discard any mussels that did not open. Let rest away from the fire.

GRILL THE TOAST

Lightly brush both sides of the bread slices with the olive oil. Grill, turning once or twice, until lightly charred and crispy, just a minute or so each side. Remove from the heat and rub each slice with the garlic clove. Smear each slice with a spoonful of roast garlic anchovy butter.

Divide the basil between bowls. Ladle equal portions of steamed mussels and broth into the bowls. Top with a slice or two of toast. Garnish with reserved basil sprigs.

SERVES 4 TO 6

SPECIAL EQUIPMENT NEEDED: large cast-iron Dutch oven

ROASTED GARLIC ANCHOVY BUTTER

2 heads of garlic

1 cup (250 mL) salted butter, softened

6 anchovy fillets, finely minced and smeared into a paste with the side of a knife

Zest and juice of 1 lemon

2 tablespoons (30 mL) minced fresh flat-leaf or curly parsley

TOMATO BASIL BROTH

2 tablespoons (30 mL) olive oil

1 large yellow or white onion, finely diced

1 large or 2 small carrots, peeled and finely diced

4 garlic cloves, finely minced

½ teaspoon (2 mL) red chili flakes

½ teaspoon (2 mL) sea salt

1 cup (250 mL) red or white wine (any type)

1 can (28 ounces/796 mL) diced or crushed tomatoes

Leaves and tender stems from 1 large bunch of fresh basil, a few sprigs reserved for garnish

IRON-STEAMED MUSSELS

5 pounds (2.25 kg) fresh mussels, rinsed well and beards removed

FIRE TOAST

12 thick slices of your favourite rustic bread

Olive oil, for brushing

1 or 2 large garlic cloves, peeled

IRON STEAMING
Cast-Iron Cooking Method

A cast-iron Dutch oven with a heavy lid makes a perfect steamer. The weight of the lid easily locks tenderizing moisture and high-temperature steam within the vessel where it tenderizes vegetables and rapidly cooks other ingredients, such as fresh mussels or other shellfish.

SALMON BURGERS WITH SRIRACHA PICKLED RED ONIONS

Light, juicy salmon burgers loaded with rich flavour and pleasantly sweet and spicy pickled red onions. A deliciously memorable sandwich for your next cookout.

BUILD A FIRE
Build and tend an active fire in your firepit, bringing to medium-high heat with no live flame and a growing bed of glowing hot coals. Position a grill grate directly over the fire. Alternatively, light your charcoal grill or fire up your gas grill to its highest setting.

MAKE THE SALMON BURGERS
Combine the salmon, dill, and pickled red onions in a food processor. Pulse for a few seconds each time, just until the mixture is a bit chunky and just comes together. Do not purée. Divide the mixture into 4 equal portions and shape into thick patties. The burgers may seem like they'll fall apart, but they'll firm up as they cook through. Place each patty on a separate square of parchment paper. Cook immediately or refrigerate until the fire is ready.

GRILL AND BUILD THE SALMON BURGERS
Stoke the fire and wait just until the damaging flames die down, while the fire's fiercest heat remains in its glowing active embers. Invert the burgers onto the grill with the parchment still attached. Remove the paper and discard. Sear the burgers over the fire until golden brown on the bottom, just 2 or 3 minutes. Flip them over and brown the second side, a few minutes longer.

While the burgers are cooking, toast the burger buns cut side down over the fire.

Transfer the salmon burgers to the bottom of each bun. Top with a leaf or two of lettuce, a few tomato slices, and a tangle of sriracha pickled red onions. Finish with the bun tops.

SERVES 4

SALMON BURGERS
1 pound (450 g) skinless salmon fillets, cubed
Leaves and tender stems from 1 bunch of fresh dill (about 2 cups/500 mL)
½ cup (125 mL) Sriracha Pickled Red Onions (page 258), minced
1 teaspoon (5 mL) sea salt

BURGER BUILD
4 soft burger buns, split
1 head of Bibb lettuce, leaves separated
2 large ripe tomatoes, thinly sliced
Sriracha Pickled Red Onions (page 258)

FLAMELESS HIGH HEAT
Cooking Fire Stage

That stage of a well-built active cooking fire when the initial flames have died down and the high heat of the active glowing embers remains. High searing heat that easily roasts and browns ingredients without the damaging effects of direct flame contact.

HAY-SMOKED SALMON WITH MARITIME MUSTARD PICKLES

Hay smoking salmon is a quick way to enjoy the fragrance of smoked salmon, finished with the unmistakable smoky perfume of fresh hay. Most salmon-smoking techniques require days of patient smoking with hardwood, but hay adds an immediate burst of distinctive last-minute flavour and fragrance.

BUILD A FIRE

Build and tend a wood or charcoal fire in a ceramic kamado-style grill or other covered grill or barbecue, bringing to medium-high heat with a thick bed of glowing hot coals. Position a lightly oiled semicircular grill grate directly over the high heat to allow direct access to the fire while you smoke.

HAY-SMOKE THE SALMON

Season the salmon fillets with salt and pepper. Place the fillets on the grate over the highest heat, add a handful of hay to the coals, and grill until the bottom is browned, 2 minutes or so. Working quickly, flip the fillets over and cover the coals with 6 inches (15 cm) or so of the hay. Within seconds it will ignite. Immediately close the lid and the top and bottom vents. Wait 10 minutes as the aromatic hay smoke flavours the fish as it finishes cooking. Transfer the fillets to a serving platter or plate. Top each fillet with a dollop of maritime mustard pickles. Serve immediately.

SERVES 4

SPECIAL EQUIPMENT NEEDED: ceramic kamado-style grill or other covered grill or barbecue; semicircular grill grate; an armful of fresh organic timothy hay from a local farmer or pet store

4 skinless salmon fillets (5 to 6 ounces/ 140 to 170 g each)
Sea salt
Freshly ground black pepper
1 cup (250 mL) Maritime Mustard Pickles (page 258)

HAY SMOKING
Smoking Method

Smoking and flavouring with the distinctive aromatic perfume of fresh fragrant hay, a herbaceous smoke that's very different from wood smoke. A brief last-second smoking method, since dry hay is not a reliable long-term heat source.

CEDAR-PLANKED SALMON WITH FENNEL SEED GLAZE AND FENNEL SALAD

A different yet practical way to cook salmon while flavouring it with aromatic smouldering cedar. An appetizingly simple glaze perfumed with fennel seed and a condiment salad of crisp raw fennel and bright lemon.

MAKE THE FENNEL SEED GLAZE

In a small bowl, whisk together the mustard, mayonnaise, honey, fennel seeds, and salt. Reserve.

BUILD A FIRE

Build and tend a wood or charcoal fire in a ceramic kamado-style grill or other covered grill or barbecue, bringing to medium-high heat with a thick bed of glowing hot coals. Position 2 supportive rods or a grill grate directly over the fire. Alternatively, light your charcoal grill or fire up your gas grill to its highest setting.

PREP THE CEDAR SHINGLE

Place the cedar shingle on the rods or grate and grill until one side is smoking and lightly charred. Remove from the fire and flip over. Position the salmon fillet on the charred shingle, with the thicker end of the salmon over the thinner end of the shingle. Season with salt and pepper. Evenly spread the fennel seed glaze over the top of the salmon.

COOK THE SALMON

Position the cedar shingle with the salmon on the grate over the fire. Close the lid and lower the heat, adjusting the top and bottom vents to low position. Cook, infusing the salmon with cedar smoke, until the glaze is browned and bubbling and the fish is cooked through, 20 minutes. The salmon is done when an instant-read thermometer registers at least 140°F (60°C).

MAKE THE FENNEL SALAD

When the salmon is almost done, toss together the fennel, minced fennel fronds, lemon zest and juice, olive oil, preserved lemon purée, and salt.

Serve the salmon topped with the salad.

SERVES 4 TO 6

SPECIAL EQUIPMENT NEEDED: an untreated cedar shingle about 7 inches (18 cm) by 17½ inches (44 cm); ceramic kamado-style grill or other covered grill or barbecue; digital instant-read thermometer

FENNEL SEED GLAZE

2 tablespoons (30 mL) yellow mustard
1 tablespoon (15 mL) mayonnaise
1 tablespoon (15 mL) pure liquid honey
1 tablespoon (15 mL) fennel seeds
1 teaspoon (5 mL) sea salt

CEDAR-PLANKED SALMON

1 skinless centre-cut or head end salmon fillet (2 pounds/900 g; do not use thinner tail section)
Sea salt
Freshly ground black pepper

FENNEL SALAD

1 fennel bulb, trimmed, cored, and very thinly sliced lengthwise on a mandoline, fronds minced
Zest and juice of 1 lemon
2 tablespoons (30 mL) extra-virgin olive oil
1 tablespoon (15 mL) Preserved Lemon Purée (page 257)
1 teaspoon (5 mL) sea salt

CEDAR PLANKING
Basic Fire Kitchen Method

Using a plank of aromatic wood or a standard cedar shingle to support an ingredient over a live fire, protecting it from the damaging direct heat, allowing the wood to smoulder, even ignite, and add smoky flavours. Inspired by the ancient need to cook without metal. Particularly effective in a closed kettle-style barbecue where the cedar is held at a smoulder without bursting into flames.

IRON-SEARED SALMON WITH FIRE-ROASTED ROMESCO SAUCE

A preheated cast-iron skillet is the secret to many chefs' perfectly cooked salmon with its crispy exterior and tender, juicy centre. Romesco is the classic pungent condiment of Spanish seafood and vegetable cookery.

BUILD A FIRE

Build and tend an active fire in your firepit, bringing to highest heat with lots of live flame. If not using a chili roaster basket, position a lightly oiled grill grate directly over the fire.

ROAST THE CHILIES

Fill the roaster basket with the chili peppers and position over the live flames. Roast, turning constantly, until softened, fragrant, and lightly charred, 15 minutes or so. Alternatively, grill on the grate, turning frequently. Transfer the chilies to a large baking pan and let rest until cool enough to handle. Carefully tug away and discard the stems and seed pods.

MAKE THE FIRE-ROASTED ROMESCO SAUCE

Transfer the chili peppers to a food processor. Add the garlic and process until smooth. Add the parsley, almonds, olive oil, sherry vinegar, paprika, salt, and chili flakes. Process until a smooth paste forms. Transfer to a small bowl and reserve.

SEAR THE SALMON

Fan the flames and position a large cast-iron skillet over the highest heat. Tend the fire and heat the skillet to 500°F (260°C) or so. For best results use a surface thermometer. Season the salmon fillets with salt and pepper. Pour the grapeseed oil into the hot pan and carefully position the salmon fillets in the sizzling pan. Sear until browned and crispy on the bottom, 3 to 4 minutes. Carefully turn and continue until the second side is browned and crispy, 3 to 4 minutes more.

Serve with lots of fire-roasted romesco sauce and an array of sides and salads.

SERVES 4

SPECIAL EQUIPMENT NEEDED: chili roaster (see page 263); large cast-iron skillet; surface thermometer

FIRE-ROASTED ROMESCO SAUCE

2 pounds (900 g) of your favourite low- to medium-heat chili peppers (poblano, Anaheim, New Mexico, mirasol, cubanelle, espanola, or red or green bell peppers)

4 large garlic cloves, minced

Leaves and tender stems from 1 bunch of fresh flat-leaf parsley

2 cups (500 mL) toasted almonds

½ cup (125 mL) extra-virgin olive oil

¼ cup (60 mL) sherry vinegar

1 tablespoon (15 mL) smoked paprika

1 teaspoon (5 mL) sea salt

¼ teaspoon (1 mL) red chili flakes

IRON-SEARED SALMON

4 skinless salmon fillets (5 to 6 ounces/ 140 to 170 g each)

Sea salt

Freshly ground black pepper

2 tablespoons (30 mL) grapeseed oil

CHILI ROASTER
Fire Kitchen Tool

A device for roasting aromatic chilies or bell peppers to scorch away their skin and soften their flesh while adding charred flavours. A metal mesh cage is filled with fresh chilies, suspended over live flame, and rotated constantly for even cooking.

WOOD-GRILLED OCTOPUS WITH TOMATO BASIL STEW

Wood-grilled octopus is one of the world's greatest marriages of flavour and flame. Tender octopus flame-grilled for caramelized taste and crispy texture. A bright tomato stew full of mouth-watering Mediterranean flavours.

BRAISE THE OCTOPUS

In a large pot, heat the olive oil over medium heat. Add the onion, carrot, garlic, fennel seeds, coriander seeds, chili flakes, and bay leaves and cook, stirring frequently, until sizzling and fragrant but not browned, 3 or 4 minutes. Stir in the tomato paste, pour in the white wine, season with salt, and bring the mixture to a steady simmer. Add the octopus, return to a simmer, adjust the heat lower, cover tightly, and braise until a small knife inserted in the thickest tentacle meets very little resistance, an hour or so. Remove from the heat and let the octopus rest in the liquid until cool. Transfer the octopus to a tray and pat dry with paper towel. Reserve if cooking soon or refrigerate, uncovered, until firm and dry, at least 2 hours or overnight. Discard the cooking liquid.

BUILD A FIRE

Build and tend an active fire in your firepit, bringing to high searing heat with live flame and a growing bed of glowing hot coals. Position a lightly oiled grill grate directly over the fire. Alternatively, light your charcoal grill or fire up your gas grill to its highest setting. Preheat a large cast-iron skillet over the fire.

STEW THE TOMATOES

When the skillet is hot, add the tomatoes and olive oil and stir together until sizzling and juicy, 2 or 3 minutes. Add the anchovies, garlic, capers, and chili flakes and continue stirring until fragrant, a minute or two. Add the red wine and bring to a full simmer. Remove from the direct heat and let rest in a warm place near the fire. Stir in the basil and salt.

GRILL THE OCTOPUS

Place the octopus on the grill grate and grill, turning frequently, until browned, lightly charred, and crisp, 3 or 4 minutes per side. Serve with tomato basil stew.

SERVES 4 TO 6

SPECIAL EQUIPMENT NEEDED: large cast-iron skillet

WOOD-GRILLED OCTOPUS

2 tablespoons (30 mL) olive oil

1 large white or yellow onion, chopped

1 large carrot, peeled and thinly sliced

Cloves from 1 head of garlic, peeled and halved

1 tablespoon (15 mL) fennel seeds

1 tablespoon (15 mL) coriander seeds

1 teaspoon (5 mL) red chili flakes

3 bay leaves

1 can (5½ ounces/156 mL) tomato paste

1 bottle (26 ounces/750 mL) dry white wine

1 teaspoon (5 mL) sea salt

1 fresh medium octopus (3 to 4 pounds/ 1.35 to 1.8 kg), cleaned, head and tentacles separated, beak discarded

TOMATO BASIL STEW

2 pounds (900 g) cherry, grape, or baby tomatoes

1 tablespoon (15 mL) olive oil

4 anchovy fillets, minced

4 garlic cloves, very thinly sliced

¼ cup (60 mL) drained capers

¼ teaspoon (1 mL) red chili flakes

½ cup (125 mL) red wine (any type)

Leaves from 1 bunch of fresh basil

¼ teaspoon (1 mL) sea salt

BRAISE GRILLING
Fire Kitchen Method

Braising an ingredient before grilling it. Adding tenderness with slow, gentle heat before adding flavour with fierce searing heat.

CHARCOAL-SEARED TUNA WITH MISO CHILI GLAZE AND CILANTRO MINT CRUST

Fresh sustainably caught tuna, deliciously seared by the intense heat of charcoal, the surface flavoured so quickly that the heat doesn't penetrate to the cool centre. A distinctive sweet and spicy glaze, rich with chili flavours. An aromatic finishing flourish as the sticky skewers roll in freshly chopped herbs brightened with lime.

MAKE THE MISO CHILI GLAZE
In a small bowl, whisk together the vegetable oil, honey, miso, gochujang, cumin, and coriander. Reserve.

MAKE THE CILANTRO MINT CRUST
In a small bowl, gently stir together the mint, cilantro, sesame seeds, and lime zest. Reserve.

PREP THE TUNA SKEWERS
Thread 2 tuna cubes onto each skewer. Cover tightly and refrigerate until needed.

BUILD A FIRE
Build a charcoal fire in a konro, hibachi, kamado, or backyard charcoal grill. Tend to a glowing bed of fiercely hot coals. If necessary, position supportive crossbars directly over the hottest coals.

GRILL THE TUNA SKEWERS
Place the skewers directly on the supports. Vigorously fan the coals to increase their searing heat. Cook the tuna, turning frequently, just until the surface sears, a minute or so. Remove the skewers from the heat and thoroughly brush with the miso chili glaze. Return to the heat and briefly continue searing, rotating continuously, setting the glaze until bubbling and lightly charred, another minute more. Remove from the heat, brush once more with the glaze, and roll in the cilantro mint crust until evenly coated. Squeeze a sprinkle of lime juice over each skewer and serve immediately.

SERVES 4 TO 6

SPECIAL EQUIPMENT NEEDED: konro, hibachi, kamado, or backyard charcoal grill; 12 bamboo skewers, soaked in water overnight, or metal skewers

MISO CHILI GLAZE
1 tablespoon (15 mL) vegetable oil
1 tablespoon (15 mL) pure liquid honey
1 tablespoon (15 mL) red miso
1 tablespoon (15 mL) gochujang
1 teaspoon (5 mL) ground cumin
1 teaspoon (5 mL) ground coriander

CILANTRO MINT CRUST
½ cup (125 mL) fresh mint leaves and tender stems, minced
Leaves and tender stems from 1 bunch of fresh cilantro, minced
¼ cup (60 mL) sesame seeds
2 limes, zested, then cut into wedges for squeezing

TUNA SKEWERS
1½ pounds (675 g) fresh bluefin or other sustainably sourced tuna, cut into even 1-inch (2.5 cm) cubes

CHARCOAL SEARING
Charcoal Cooking Method

Using the intense heat of live charcoal to flavourfully sear the surface of an ingredient so quickly that the heat doesn't have time to penetrate to the centre and overcook the interior. A live bed of glowing charcoal is among the very hottest heat options in the fire kitchen.

WOOD-FIRED VEGETABLES

CAMPFIRE-STYLE BROWN BUTTER CAULIFLOWER

Once the protein is chosen and the cooking fire is roaring away, every fire cook needs a few reliably tasty vegetable side dishes in their repertoire to complete the meal. Cauliflower steamed tender then finished with brown butter just might become one of your simple favourites.

BUILD A FIRE

Build and tend an active fire in your firepit, bringing to medium-high heat with live flame and a growing bed of glowing hot coals. Position a grill grate directly over the fire. Alternatively, light your charcoal grill or fire up your gas grill to its highest setting.

MAKE THE CAULIFLOWER

Position a large cast-iron skillet or Dutch oven over the fire's highest heat. Add the cauliflower, 1 cup (250 mL) of the water, and the butter. Cover tightly. Cook quickly, stirring occasionally, steaming the cauliflower until tender, 5 minutes or so. Remove the lid and continue cooking, stirring frequently, until the water evaporates and the butter is sizzling and browned, 5 minutes or so. Stir in the remaining ½ cup (125 mL) water and season with nutmeg, salt, and pepper. Cover tightly and let rest in a warm place near the fire.

SERVES 4 TO 6

SPECIAL EQUIPMENT NEEDED: large cast-iron skillet or Dutch oven

1 head of cauliflower, cut into florets
1½ cups (375 mL) water, divided
¼ cup (60 mL) butter
¼ teaspoon (1 mL) nutmeg
Sea salt
Freshly ground black pepper

BROWN BUTTER FINISHING
Fire Cooking Technique

Butter is delicate and burns easily in the high-heat environment of fire cooking, so it's best used not as the primary cooking fat but as a finishing flavour. A few careful swirling moments before finishing a sizzling vegetable shows respect for the ingredient.

GRILLED CORN POLENTA

This flavourful side dish is a classic part of the fire cook's repertoire. A favourite with vegetarians, it easily accompanies any grilled protein too. A crispy crust, creamy centre, and lots of sweet corn flavour in every slice. If possible, make the polenta the day before you grill it for maximum strength.

MAKE THE POLENTA
Preheat the oven to 350°F (180°C). Pour the water into a Dutch oven or medium pot over medium-high heat. Add the garlic, bay leaf, and salt. Bring to a full simmer. Whisking constantly to prevent lumps, slowly pour in the cornmeal until dissolved in the water. Stir in the corn kernels. Transfer to the oven and bake, uncovered, stirring vigorously every 20 minutes. At the 40-minute mark, stir in the butter, then continue to bake until the cornmeal absorbs all the liquid and a thick, smooth polenta forms, another 10 minutes or so. Discard the bay leaf.

Lightly spray a 9 x 5-inch (2 L) loaf pan with oil and line with plastic wrap. Scrape the polenta into the lined pan and smooth the surface. Cover tightly with plastic wrap and refrigerate until cold and firm, at least 3 to 4 hours or overnight.

Turn the polenta out of the pan and cut evenly into 1-inch (2.5 cm) thick slices. Lay the slices close together on a baking sheet. Lightly moisten their surfaces with spray oil, turning and sliding on the tray until evenly coated.

BUILD A FIRE
Build and tend an active fire in your firepit, bringing to medium-high heat with live flame and a growing bed of glowing hot coals. Position a lightly oiled grill grate directly over the fire. Alternatively, light your charcoal grill or fire up your gas grill to its highest setting.

GRILL THE POLENTA
Place the oiled polenta on the grill grates and grill, turning occasionally, cooking each side until lightly charred and crispy on the outside and heated through, 10 minutes or so total. Transfer to a resting platter. Serve with your favourite grilled meat or fish.

MAKES 8 SLICES

SPECIAL EQUIPMENT NEEDED: cast-iron Dutch oven

4 cups (1 L) water
4 garlic cloves, finely minced
1 bay leaf
2 teaspoons (10 mL) sea salt
1 cup (250 mL) fine yellow cornmeal
1 cup (250 mL) fresh or frozen corn kernels
2 tablespoons (30 mL) butter

GRILLING POLENTA
Fire Cooking Method

Cornmeal transformed into strong polenta, then chilled, cut into firm slices, and grilled. For grilling, polenta must be crafted patiently for strength, then thoroughly chilled for accurate slicing.

CHIA LENTIL CAKES WITH COAL-ROASTED BABA GHANOUSH

Chia lentil cakes are packed with vegetarian protein and have become one of our signature dishes at the inn. A hearty plant-based centrepiece patiently crisped in a forgiving cast-iron skillet. Eggplants cooked in the glowing coals of the fire, easily softened, and memorably charred by the direct primal heat before being puréed into fragrant baba ghanoush.

PREP THE CHIA LENTIL CAKES

Heat the vegetable oil in a large skillet over medium-high heat. Add the onion and garlic and sauté until softened and fragrant but not browned, 2 or 3 minutes. Add the mushrooms, cover tightly, reduce the heat to low, and continue cooking, stirring occasionally, until the mushrooms fully release their moisture, 10 minutes or so. Stir in the brown rice, lentils, water, and bay leaf. Bring to a slow, steady simmer. Cover and continue cooking, stirring occasionally, until the rice and lentils are tender, 30 minutes. Without uncovering, remove from the heat and let rest for 10 minutes.

Discard the bay leaf. Transfer the rice and lentil mixture to a food processor. Add the chia seeds, peanut butter, miso, and soy sauce. Pulse until smooth, scraping down the sides once or twice. Transfer to a large bowl and stir in the sweet potato by hand. Cover tightly with plastic wrap and refrigerate, giving the chia seeds time to work their magic, absorbing, swelling, and strengthening the protein-rich savoury blend, at least 1 hour, ideally overnight.

Using your hands, shape the mixture into even cakes 2 inches (5 cm) thick. Reserve on a lightly oiled parchment paper–lined baking sheet until ready to cook.

BUILD A FIRE

Build and tend an active fire in your firepit, bringing to medium-high heat with live flame and a growing bed of glowing hot coals. Position a grill grate directly over the fire. Alternatively, light your charcoal grill or fire up your gas grill to its highest setting.

COAL-ROAST THE EGGPLANT

Rake a glowing bed of coals to the side of the fire. Nestle the eggplants directly into the embers, turning occasionally and repositioning over fresher coals as the heat is smothered, cooking until tender and thoroughly charred, 20 minutes or so. Remove from the fire and let rest until cool enough to handle.

SERVES 4 TO 6

SPECIAL EQUIPMENT NEEDED: 14-inch (35 cm) cast-iron skillet

CHIA LENTIL CAKES

2 tablespoons (30 mL) vegetable or olive oil, more for frying

1 yellow or white onion, finely chopped

Cloves from 1 head of garlic, finely minced

1 pound (450 g) mushrooms (a single type or a blend of varieties such as cremini, portobello, oyster, chanterelle, and king), sliced

1 cup (250 mL) brown rice

1 cup (250 mL) dried green lentils

2½ cups (625 mL) water

1 cup (250 mL) white chia seeds

½ cup (125 mL) smoked peanut butter or your favourite nut butter

2 tablespoons (30 mL) red miso

2 tablespoons (30 mL) soy sauce

1 sweet potato, peeled and grated

COAL-ROASTED BABA GHANOUSH

2 large globe or Italian eggplants (about 2 pounds/900 g total)

¼ cup (60 mL) tahini

¼ cup (60 mL) natural plain full-fat yogurt or plain Greek yogurt

Zest and juice of 1 lemon

2 garlic cloves, finely grated with a microplane or finely minced

1 teaspoon (5 mL) salt

½ teaspoon (2 mL) ground cumin

½ teaspoon (2 mL) red chili flakes

Recipe continues

MAKE THE COAL-ROASTED BABA GHANOUSH

Discard all, some, or none of the charred skin of the eggplants. Transfer the flesh and bits of blackened skin to a food processor. Add the tahini, yogurt, lemon zest and juice, garlic, salt, cumin, and chili flakes. Purée until smooth. Taste and adjust salt as needed. Reserve or transfer to a resealable container and refrigerate for up to 3 days.

COOK THE CHIA LENTIL CAKES

Preheat a 14-inch (35 cm) cast-iron skillet on the grill grate over medium-high heat. Swirl and coat evenly with a splash of vegetable oil. Place the cakes in the hot skillet and lightly fry, occasionally gently shaking, until browned on the bottom, 5 minutes or so. Carefully turn and continue until the second side is cooked, 5 minutes or so. Serve with coal-roasted baba ghanoush.

CHARRED VEGETABLE SKIN
Fire Kitchen Flavour

Many vegetables are cooked whole, insulated from the direct heat of the fire by their protective skins. Some charred skins are horribly bitter or tough and chewy, but others are quite aromatic. Eggplant skin is so tasty that it's often included in classic baba ghanoush.

PLANCHA POTATOES

This is one of our favourite ways to cook Prince Edward Island's legendary potatoes. A perfectly golden crispy-crunchy crust and an impossibly creamy centre. Our version of the holy grail that restaurant empires have been built on. Extreme textural contrast and rich, buttery flavour. The industry standard is to partially cook the potatoes at a lower heat, nudge the interior's doneness so the exterior can crisp at a higher heat later. At the inn we use local high-starch potatoes, fragrantly simmered until nearly mashable, the consistent slow heat of cast-iron and butter, lots and lots of butter.

PREP THE POTATOES

Bring a large pot of salted water to a rolling boil. Add the potato slices and bay leaves, stir gently, adjust the heat, and slowly boil, uncovered, until very tender and the flesh splits, 25 minutes or so. Remove from the heat. With a slotted spoon or small wire mesh strainer, carefully transfer the potato slices to a lightly oiled baking sheet and let rest until cooled.

BUILD A FIRE

Build and tend a slow fire in your firepit, bringing to medium-low heat with a thick bed of glowing coals. Position a plancha or large cast-iron skillet directly over the coals. Alternatively, position a plancha in a warm place near or above an active live fire. Heat the plancha, adjusting the coals and the plancha's position until the surface is uniformly 300°F (150°C). For best results use a surface thermometer.

ROAST THE POTATOES

Vigorously rub the plancha with a lightly oiled cloth. Add about a third of the butter and swirl until melted and evenly coating the plancha. Snugly position the potatoes on the hot surface and slowly roast until uniformly golden brown, crispy, and caramelized on the bottom, about 30 minutes. Carefully turn the potatoes, add another third of the butter, and continue slowly cooking until the second side is as crispy as the first, another 30 minutes. Add the remaining butter in the last few minutes, turning the golden-brown potatoes frequently, butter-basting them to the finish line. Lightly season with salt and pepper. The insides will still be creamy and smooth. Serve with your favourite wood-fired masterpiece.

SERVES 4 TO 6

SPECIAL EQUIPMENT NEEDED: large plancha or cast-iron skillet; surface thermometer

4 extra-large Russet Burbank high-starch baking potatoes, unpeeled, cut into 1-inch (2.5 cm) thick rounds
4 bay leaves
8 tablespoons (125 mL) butter, divided
Sea salt
Freshly ground black pepper

CHARRED VEGETABLE SKIN
Fire Kitchen Flavour

Many vegetables are cooked whole, insulated from the direct heat of the fire by their protective skins. Some charred skins are horribly bitter or tough and chewy, but others are quite aromatic.

IRON CAULIFLOWER WITH PICKLED CAULIFLOWER RELISH

The versatility of cauliflower is showcased in this side dish of contrasting textures, colours, and flavours. Patiently browned cauliflower florets caramelized with the even, consistent heat of cast iron and deeply flavoured with a splash of animal fat. A spicy improvised relish made from the crunchy raw cauliflower trimmings.

PREP THE CAULIFLOWER
Remove the leaves. Cut the cauliflower into 2-inch (5 cm) florets. Reserve. Dice the stalk and trimmings and reserve separately.

MAKE THE PICKLED CAULIFLOWER RELISH
In a small dry sauté pan over medium-high heat, toast the fennel seeds, shaking constantly, until fragrant, a minute or so. Pour in the olive oil and add the jalapeño, oregano, and chili flakes. Continue cooking, stirring gently, until sizzling. Remove from the heat. Whisk in the garlic, mustard, cider vinegar, and salt until smooth. Transfer to a small food processor and add the reserved cauliflower trimmings. Pulse, scraping down the sides once or twice with a rubber spatula, until coarsely chopped into a uniform relish. Transfer to a mason jar or small bowl and reserve at room temperature or refrigerate for up to 1 month.

BUILD A FIRE
Build and tend an active fire in your firepit, bringing to medium-high heat with live flame and a growing bed of glowing hot coals. Position a grill grate directly over the fire. Alternatively, light your charcoal grill or fire up your gas grill to its highest setting.

ROAST THE CAULIFLOWER
In a large bowl, toss the cauliflower florets with the fat, salt, and pepper until evenly coated. Transfer to a large cast-iron skillet and cook, shaking frequently, stirring, and settling the sizzling pan, until the cauliflower is golden brown all over and tender, 20 minutes or so. Remove from the heat and serve topped with the cauliflower relish.

SERVES 4 TO 6

SPECIAL EQUIPMENT NEEDED: large cast-iron skillet

IRON CAULIFLOWER
1 large head of cauliflower
2 tablespoons (30 mL) melted animal fat (beef, chicken, pork, turkey, or duck) or vegetable oil
Kosher salt
Freshly ground black pepper

PICKLED CAULIFLOWER RELISH
1 tablespoon (15 mL) fennel seeds
2 tablespoons (30 mL) olive oil
1 jalapeño pepper, stem, seeds, and pith discarded, minced
1 teaspoon (5 mL) dried oregano
¼ teaspoon (1 mL) red chili flakes
2 garlic cloves, grated with a microplane into a paste
1 tablespoon (15 mL) yellow mustard
¼ cup (60 mL) apple cider vinegar
½ teaspoon (2 mL) kosher salt
Reserved cauliflower trimmings (from above)

ANIMAL FAT
Fire Kitchen Ingredient

Rendered animal fat has long been valued for its versatility, affordability, and incomparable flavour. Uniquely, animal fat can also endure very high cooking temperatures, making it very effective for consistent browning. A key ingredient in vegetable-forward cooking, allowing for the flavour of meat without its heft.

BLISTERED PEAS WITH UMAMI BUTTER

Fresh peas fiercely seared so quickly that they lightly char while staying bright green, tender, and juicy, an impossible task without a genius cooking tool. Garden-fresh flavour, searing heat unlocked by the cook, and a deeply savoury dressing elevating the peas with umami-rich flavours.

MAKE THE UMAMI BUTTER

Toss the butter into a small saucepan over medium-high heat. Swirl gently as it melts, steams, foams, and eventually lightly browns. Stir in the garlic and chili flakes. Remove from the heat, swirl gently until the garlic is fragrant, then stir in the miso, fish sauce, and Worcestershire sauce. Reserve.

BUILD A FIRE

Build and tend an active fire in your firepit, bringing to highest heat with lots of live flame.

BLISTER THE PEAS

In a large bowl, toss the snow and snap peas with the vegetable oil until evenly coated. Transfer to the grilling basket and position the basket directly within the fiercest flames, gently tossing, constantly moving, until the peas are bright green and tender, even lightly charred, just 60 seconds. Return the peas to the bowl and toss with the umami butter. Serve immediately.

SERVES 4 TO 6

SPECIAL EQUIPMENT NEEDED: wire-mesh grilling basket; heavy-duty work gloves

UMAMI BUTTER

2 tablespoons (30 mL) butter
2 garlic cloves, finely grated with a microplane or finely minced
¼ teaspoon (1 mL) red chili flakes
1 tablespoon (15 mL) yellow miso
1 tablespoon (15 mL) fish sauce
1 teaspoon (5 mL) Worcestershire sauce

BLISTERED PEAS

1 pound (450 g) snow peas
1 pound (450 g) snap peas
1 teaspoon (5 mL) vegetable oil

GRILLING BASKET
Fire Kitchen Tool

A wire-mesh basket allowing delicate vegetables to be quickly roasted within the searing heat of live flames. A tool to avoid impractical individual flipping or turning of smaller ingredients.

FIRE-KISSED BROCCOLI SALAD WITH BROCCOLI HUMMUS

Humble broccoli florets roasted crispy within the roaring flames, lightly charred by the fire, barely tender, even crunchy. The trimmed stalks and stems sweetly steamed soft then puréed into a rich, tangy hummus.

PREP THE BROCCOLI

Cut the broccoli into 2-inch (5 cm) florets. In a large bowl, toss together the florets and vegetable oil. Reserve. Dice the stalk and trimmings and reserve separately.

MAKE THE BROCCOLI HUMMUS

Bring a small saucepan of lightly salted water to a simmer. Add the diced broccoli and cook briefly until tender, 3 minutes or so. Drain well. In a food processor, combine the diced broccoli, chickpeas, tahini, olive oil, lemon zest and juice, garlic, cumin, salt, and pepper. Purée until smooth. Reserve.

BUILD A FIRE

Build and tend an active fire in your firepit, bringing to highest heat with lots of live flame. If not using a grilling basket, place a wire-mesh cooling rack over a grill grate.

CHAR THE BROCCOLI AND FINISH THE SALAD

Transfer the broccoli florets to a grilling basket (reserve the bowl) and position directly within the flames, gently tossing, constantly moving, until the edges are lightly charred, even crispy, and the florets are tender, 3 minutes. Alternatively, position the florets in a single layer on the wire mesh cooling rack and grill, turning frequently. Transfer the charred broccoli to the bowl. Add the soy sauce and sesame oil and toss evenly.

Scrape the hummus onto the centre of a serving platter, smoothing the surface. Arrange the broccoli on top of the hummus and serve.

SERVES 4 TO 6

SPECIAL EQUIPMENT NEEDED: wire-mesh grilling basket; heavy-duty work gloves

FIRE-KISSED BROCCOLI SALAD

2 bunches of broccoli (about 2 pounds/ 900 g total)
1 tablespoon (15 mL) vegetable oil
1 tablespoon (15 mL) soy sauce
1 teaspoon (5 mL) sesame oil

BROCCOLI HUMMUS

Reserved broccoli trimmings (from above)
1 can (19 ounces/540 mL) chickpeas, drained and rinsed
½ cup (125 mL) tahini
¼ cup (60 mL) high-quality extra-virgin olive oil
Zest and juice of 2 lemons
4 garlic cloves, finely grated with a microplane
1 tablespoon (15 mL) ground cumin
1 teaspoon (5 mL) sea salt
Freshly ground black pepper

FIRE KISSING
Fire Cooking Method

Briefly cooking delicate ingredients directly within the roaring flames of an active fire with heat so intense that surfaces sear and brown so quickly that centres don't overcook.

GRILLED CARROTS WITH ARUGULA, PUMPKIN SEED, AND GOAT CHEESE PESTO

Sweet carrots tenderized by a brief boil before being flavourfully finished over the fierce flames of a grill. A bright pesto tangy with goat cheese and peppery arugula.

MAKE THE ARUGULA, PUMPKIN SEED, AND GOAT CHEESE PESTO
In a food processor, combine the arugula, pumpkin seeds, garlic, and salt. Process to a smooth purée, scraping down the sides once or twice. Add the goat cheese and process until well combined. Reserve or transfer to a resealable container and refrigerate for up to 3 days.

PARCOOK THE CARROTS
Bring a large pot of heavily salted water to a rolling boil over medium-high heat. Add the carrots and cook just long enough for the heat to penetrate and lightly relax their texture, 4 minutes. Drain well and let rest until the fire is ready.

BUILD A FIRE
Build and tend a slow fire in your firepit, bringing to medium heat with no live flame and a growing bed of glowing hot coals. Position a lightly oiled grill grate directly over the fire. Alternatively, light your charcoal grill or fire up your gas grill to its medium setting.

GRILL THE CARROTS
Neatly arrange the carrots on a baking sheet. Drizzle with vegetable oil, season with salt and pepper, and toss to evenly coat. Position the carrots perpendicular to the grill grates and sear, turning occasionally, grilling until lightly charred and tender, about 10 minutes.

Transfer the carrots to a serving platter. Top with the arugula, pumpkin seed, and goat cheese pesto. Garnish with reserved carrot fronds.

SERVES 4 TO 6

ARUGULA, PUMPKIN SEED, AND GOAT CHEESE PESTO
5 ounces (140 g) fresh arugula
1 cup (250 mL) unsalted roasted pumpkin seeds
2 garlic cloves, thinly sliced
1 teaspoon (5 mL) salt
4 ounces (115 g) soft goat cheese

GRILLED CARROTS
1 large bunch of slender multi-coloured carrots (2 to 3 pounds/900 g to 1.35 kg), unpeeled, small carrots whole, larger carrots cut in half lengthwise, a few fronds reserved for garnish
2 tablespoons (30 mL) vegetable oil
Sea salt
Freshly ground black pepper

PARCOOKING
Basic Cooking Method

To improve the texture of an ingredient by briefly cooking it in advance before finishing it with a different cooking method. To minimize time spent at damaging high temperatures by first cooking at a lower controlled temperature, then searing and caramelizing at a higher temperature.

GRILLED RATATOUILLE SALAD WITH ROASTED GARLIC TOMATO DRESSING AND FRESH BASIL

The summer-garden flavours of classic Provençal vegetable stew transformed into a bright salad by lightly grilling the traditional vegetables to tenderness. A fresh dressing of fragrant tomato purée, mellow roasted garlic, and fresh basil leaves.

BUILD A FIRE
Build and tend an active fire in your firepit, bringing to medium-high heat with live flame and a growing bed of glowing hot coals. Position a grill grate directly over the fire. Alternatively, light your charcoal grill or fire up your gas grill to its highest setting.

MAKE THE ROASTED GARLIC TOMATO DRESSING
Position the garlic heads to the side of the main fire and slowly roast, turning occasionally, until softened, charred, and the juices begin to ooze from the top, 20 to 30 minutes. Let rest away from the fire until cool enough to handle.

Once the roasted garlic is cool, use a serrated knife to slice off the tops. Squeeze the soft cloves into a high-speed blender. Add the tomatoes, olive oil, lemon zest and juice, anchovies, mustard, hot sauce, and salt. Purée until smooth and thick. Reserve.

GRILL THE RATATOUILLE AND FINISH THE SALAD
Without mixing the vegetables together, place the bell peppers, fennel, eggplant, red onions, zucchini, and squash on a large baking sheet. Drizzle with the olive oil and season with salt. Use your hands to evenly coat the vegetables.

Place the bell peppers and fennel on the grill first. Cook, turning occasionally, until brightened and barely tender, 5 minutes or so. Transfer to a medium bowl, cover tightly with foil, and let rest. (The vegetables' retained heat will continue to soften them.)

Position the eggplant slices on the grill and cook, turning occasionally, until lightly browned and their centres are soft, creamy, and translucent, 5 minutes or so. Stack the eggplant slices on a resting platter. Carefully grill the red onions, preserving their nestled rings, turning occasionally, until lightly roasted and fully tender. Transfer to the platter. Grill the zucchini and squash, flipping occasionally, until lightly roasted and just barely tender. Transfer to the platter.

Cut the various grilled vegetables into bite-size pieces. Transfer to a large bowl. Add the basil leaves and roasted garlic tomato dressing. Toss lightly to combine.

SERVES 6 TO 8

ROASTED GARLIC TOMATO DRESSING
2 heads of garlic, unpeeled

2 large ripe juicy heirloom tomatoes (about 1 pound/450 g), halved crosswise

¼ cup (60 mL) extra-virgin olive oil

Zest and juice of 1 lemon

4 anchovy fillets

1 teaspoon (5 mL) Dijon mustard

½ teaspoon (2 mL) of your favourite hot sauce

½ teaspoon (2 mL) sea salt

GRILLED RATATOUILLE SALAD
2 red bell peppers, halved, stems, seeds, and pith discarded, flattened

1 fennel bulb, trimmed, halved, cored, and cut into ½-inch (1 cm) thick slices

1 large Italian-style eggplant, trimmed and sliced into ½-inch (1 cm) thick rounds

2 red onions, sliced into ½-inch (1 cm) thick rounds

2 zucchini, trimmed and halved lengthwise

2 yellow squash, trimmed and halved lengthwise

½ cup (125 mL) extra-virgin olive oil

1 teaspoon (5 mL) sea salt

Leaves and tender stems from 1 large bunch of fresh basil

GRILLING VEGETABLES
Fire Cooking Method

Utilizing the fierce heat of live flame to quickly and precisely transform the texture of tender vegetables without ruinously charring their surface and dulling their fresh flavours. A technique relying on textural doneness cues rather than visual ones.

GRILLED SWEET POTATOES WITH MAPLE MUSTARD GLAZE

Nutritionally dense sweet potatoes are simple to grill and easily absorb the smoky flavours of the fire while they cook alone or next to the main dish. A spicy sweet last-second glaze adds a beautiful finishing flavour.

BUILD A FIRE

Build and tend an active fire in your firepit, bringing to medium heat with little live flame and a growing bed of glowing hot coals. Position a grill grate directly over the fire. Alternatively, light your charcoal grill or fire up your gas grill to its highest setting.

GRILL THE SWEET POTATOES

Layer the sweet potatoes on a baking sheet, drizzle with the vegetable oil, and season with salt. Turn and mix until evenly oiled and seasoned. Place the sweet potatoes on the grill and cook, turning occasionally, until tender, evenly browned, and lightly charred, 20 minutes or so. The first 10 minutes will be uneventful but halfway along the cooking will accelerate.

MAKE THE MAPLE MUSTARD GLAZE AND FINISH

In a small bowl, whisk together the maple syrup, mustard, and soy sauce. When the grilled sweet potatoes are tender, brush with the glaze a few times, turning frequently, without burning, a few minutes longer, until all the sauce is used.

SERVES 4 TO 6

GRILLED SWEET POTATOES
2 large sweet potatoes, unpeeled, sliced into ½-inch (1 cm) thick rounds
2 tablespoons (30 mL) vegetable oil
Sea salt

MAPLE MUSTARD GLAZE
¼ cup (60 mL) maple syrup
¼ cup (60 mL) grainy mustard
1 teaspoon (5 mL) soy sauce

FINISHING GLAZE
Fire Cooking Method

Applying a sweetened sauce at the end of cooking to glaze and briefly finish the main ingredient without burning the sauce through prolonged cooking of its sugars.

EMBER-ROASTED ACORN SQUASH
WITH TARRAGON APPLESAUCE

Acorn squash must have been created by the god of fire to show how easy it is to ember-roast. This is a spectacularly simple way to add a vegetable side dish of fire-fuelled flavour to your next cooking fire. Traditional applesauce brightened with tangy tarragon into deliciously savoury and sweet filling for the juicy centres.

MAKE THE TARRAGON APPLESAUCE

In a large saucepan, stir together the apples, lemon zest and juice, brown sugar, liqueur, Worcestershire sauce, and salt. Bring the mixture to a simmer over medium heat. Cover tightly, adjust the heat to the lowest setting, and continue cooking, stirring frequently, until the apples fully soften and collapse, 10 minutes or so. Purée until smooth with an immersion blender or in a food processor. Stir in the tarragon. Reserve or transfer to a resealable container and refrigerate for up to 5 days.

BUILD A FIRE

Build and tend a fire in your firepit, bringing to a thick bed of glowing hot active coals to one side and an active fire to the other side for replenishing the coals.

EMBER-ROAST THE SQUASH

Nestle the squash directly into the glowing coals and roast, turning and moving occasionally to a hotter position as the old one cools down, until the outer skin is evenly charred and the squash is tender, 30 minutes. You'll feel the doneness of the squash progress as it cooks, and eventually it will soften. Transfer to a platter and let rest for 10 minutes.

Halve each squash lengthwise and scoop out and discard the seeds and stringy bits. Season with salt and pepper. Add a few heaping spoonfuls of the tarragon applesauce to each hollow and top with a sprig of tarragon. Serve with remaining applesauce on the side.

SERVES 4

TARRAGON APPLESAUCE

4 apples (Honeycrisp, McIntosh, Cortland, Jonagold, or Granny Smith), unpeeled, cored, and chopped

Zest and juice of 1 lemon

¼ cup (60 mL) firmly packed brown sugar

¼ cup (60 mL) Pernod, Sambuca, ouzo, or other anise liqueur

1 teaspoon (5 mL) Worcestershire sauce

¼ teaspoon (1 mL) sea salt

Leaves and tender stems from 1 bunch of fresh tarragon, lightly chopped, a few sprigs reserved for garnish

EMBER-ROASTED ACORN SQUASH

2 acorn squash (about 1 pound/450 g each)

Sea salt

Freshly ground black pepper

EMBER-ROASTING VEGETABLES
Fire Cooking Method

The flavourfully fortuitous combination of a thick bed of glowing hot coals and the thick, durable skin of various vegetables. Cooking vegetables directly within the glowing hot coals of an active or dying fire.

WOOD-ROASTED BRUSSELS SPROUTS
WITH NDUJA DRESSING AND PICKLED RAISINS

Brussels sprouts are my favourite vegetable in the wood oven. Their shape is perfect for roasting, the surface easily charred as the centre cooks through, and their slightly bitter taste is enhanced by the wood-fired flavours. Nduja is a spreadable spicy Italian sausage that easily dresses the roasted sprouts. Pickled raisins add just the right bright balancing sweet and sour finishing flavour.

MAKE THE PICKLED RAISINS

In a small saucepan, combine the sugar, red wine vinegar, and salt and bring to a steady simmer over medium heat. Stir in the raisins, cover tightly, and remove from the heat. Reserve.

BUILD A FIRE

Build and tend an active fire in your wood oven, bringing to high roasting temperature and a bed of glowing hot coals. Push the fire to the back, clearing a roasting area to the front. Monitor the cooking temperature with a high-temperature ovenproof thermometer or infrared thermometer. Tend the fire, bringing the oven to 500°F (260°C) or more. Preheat a 16-inch (40 cm) cast-iron skillet in the wood oven. Alternatively, preheat your indoor oven with the skillet.

ROAST THE BRUSSELS SPROUTS AND FINISH

In a large bowl, toss together the Brussels sprouts, vegetable oil, and salt. Remove the skillet from the oven and tumble in the Brussels sprouts. Return to the oven and roast, rotating occasionally for even cooking, shaking, stirring, and settling the pan, until the sprouts are beautifully browned and tender, 15 to 20 minutes. Remove from the oven and toss with the nduja and pickled raisins.

SERVES 4 TO 6

SPECIAL EQUIPMENT NEEDED:
wood oven; 16-inch (40 cm) cast-iron skillet; high-temperature ovenproof thermometer or infrared thermometer; digital instant-read thermometer

PICKLED RAISINS
¼ cup (60 mL) sugar
¼ cup (60 mL) red wine vinegar
Pinch of sea salt
½ cup (125 mL) dark raisins

BRUSSELS SPROUTS AND NDUJA DRESSING
2 pounds (900 g) Brussels sprouts, trimmed
1 tablespoon (15 mL) vegetable oil or bacon fat
Sea salt
2 ounces (55 g) nduja (soft, spicy salami), at room temperature

WOOD-ROASTING VEGETABLES
Fire Cooking Method

Roasting vegetables in a wood oven with a live fire. A cooking temperature range from low and slow to fast and fierce. Imbuing perfectly cooked vegetables with the flavours of a wood fire.

BLISTERED TOMATOES WITH BASIL, FETA, AND SRIRACHA PICKLED RED ONIONS

Sweet, juicy tomatoes deeply flavoured by the intense searing heat of a grilling basket or preheated cast-iron skillet. Heat so intense that it exquisitely chars the tomato skin, barely warming the flesh before any precious juices are lost. The distinctive flavour of flame. A warm salad tossed with bright, aromatic basil, salty feta, and spicy pickled red onions.

BUILD A FIRE

Build and tend an active fire in your firepit, bringing to highest heat with lots of live flame. If not using a grilling basket, preheat a large cast-iron skillet on a grill grate over the fire.

BLISTER THE TOMATOES

In a large bowl, toss the tomatoes with the vegetable oil until evenly coated. Season lightly with salt and pepper. Transfer the tomatoes to a grilling basket (reserve the bowl) and position it directly within the fiercest flames, gently tossing, constantly moving, until bright red and the skin has blistered, just 60 seconds. Alternatively, transfer to the hot skillet and sear, sautéing, constantly shaking and shivering the pan, until the tomatoes are sizzling hot and blistered, even lightly charred, just a minute or so. Transfer the blistered tomatoes to the bowl.

FINISH THE TOMATOES

Add the basil, feta, and sriracha pickled red onions and their juices to the bowl of tomatoes and lightly toss until evenly combined. Serve immediately.

SERVES 4 TO 6

SPECIAL EQUIPMENT NEEDED: wire-mesh grilling basket or large cast-iron skillet; heavy-duty work gloves

2 pounds (900 g) assorted grape and baby tomatoes

1 teaspoon (5 mL) vegetable oil

Sea salt

Freshly ground black pepper

Leaves and tender stems from 1 bunch of fresh basil

6 ounces (170 g) feta cheese, crumbled, at room temperature

½ cup (125 mL) Sriracha Pickled Red Onions (page 258) and their juices

FLAME BLISTERING
Fire Cooking Method

Searing the surface of an ingredient until lightly blistered but not charred. Cooking with such an intense heat that the ingredient's surface roasts immediately, before the heat can penetrate and overcook the inside. An intense method that captures the special flavour of flame.

MEXICAN GRILLED CORN WITH CHILI, LIME, AND COTIJA CHEESE

Perhaps the very best way to enjoy a cob of corn, Mexican street food style, grilled and charred, then slathered with a tangy, fragrant topping. It's worth building a fire just for this treat!

MAKE THE CORN TOPPING

In a medium bowl, thoroughly whisk together the cheese, mayonnaise, crema, cilantro, chili powder, cumin, garlic, and lime zest and juice. Transfer the mixture to a shallow pan or dish large to fit a few cobs of corn. Cover tightly and reserve at room temperature.

BUILD A FIRE

Build and tend an active fire in your firepit, bringing to medium-high heat with live flame and a growing bed of glowing hot coals. Position a lightly oiled grill grate directly over the fire. Alternatively, light your charcoal grill or fire up your gas grill to its highest setting.

GRILL THE CORN

Place the corn on the grate and grill, turning occasionally with tongs, until lightly charred and tender, 10 minutes or so. Immediately transfer the corn, a few cobs at a time, to the cheese mixture and roll until generously coated. Sprinkle with a bit more cheese, chili powder, and cilantro. Serve immediately with lime wedges for squeezing.

SERVES 4 TO 8

- 1 cup (110 g) finely crumbled Cotija or feta cheese, at room temperature, plus more for serving
- ¼ cup (60 mL) mayonnaise
- ¼ cup (60 mL) Mexican crema or sour cream
- Leaves and tender stems from 1 bunch of fresh cilantro, chopped, plus more for serving
- 1 teaspoon (5 mL) ancho or guajillo chili powder, plus more for serving
- ½ teaspoon (2 mL) ground cumin
- 2 garlic cloves, finely grated with a microplane or finely minced
- 2 limes (1 zested and juiced; 1 cut into 8 wedges for serving)
- 8 sweet corncobs, shucked

GRILLING CORN
Fire Cooking Method

Cooking a whole cob of freshly shucked corn directly over a live fire until tender and flavourfully charred. A simple side dish prepared a myriad of ways around the world anytime a cooking fire is roaring in the hearth when the harvest comes in.

GRILLED CAESAR SALAD WITH ANCHOVY GARLIC DRESSING AND FIRE-TOASTED CROUTONS

The classic flavours of a delicious Caesar salad elevated by flames makes a perfect side dish for your next cooking fire. Romaine lettuce is transformed by the grill from bland supporting actor to appetizingly savoury centrepiece.

MAKE THE ANCHOVY GARLIC DRESSING

In a high-speed blender or food processor, combine the anchovies, garlic, olive oil, mayonnaise, mustard, honey, Worcestershire sauce, lemon zest and juice, and pepper. Purée, scraping down the sides once or twice with a rubber spatula, until smooth and creamy. Reserve or transfer to a resealable container and refrigerate for up to 5 days.

BUILD A FIRE

Build and tend an active fire in your firepit, bringing to medium-high heat with live flame and a growing bed of glowing hot coals. Position a lightly oiled grill grate directly over the fire. Alternatively, light your charcoal grill or fire up your gas grill to its highest setting.

FIRE-TOAST THE CROUTONS

Place the bread slices in a single layer on a baking sheet. Lightly brush the surfaces with water, flipping over and moistening the bread. Repeat with the olive oil, evenly brushing the surfaces. (These two brushing steps help the croutons become simultaneously crisp and chewy.) Tend the fire to medium-low heat. Position the bread slices on the grill and toast, turning occasionally, until evenly and lightly browned. Remove and vigorously and evenly rub the surfaces with raw garlic cloves. Lightly season with salt and pepper. Reserve.

GRILL THE ROMAINE AND ASSEMBLE THE SALAD

Place the romaine wedges on a baking sheet. Thoroughly brush each wedge with anchovy garlic dressing. Place the wedges on the grate and briefly grill each side, turning frequently, until lightly browned, a minute or two total. Transfer the grilled wedges to a serving platter or individual plates. Using a vegetable peeler, peel long ribbons of Parmesan over each serving. Top with fire-toasted croutons and freshly ground pepper.

SERVES 4

ANCHOVY GARLIC DRESSING
1 can (2 ounces/50 g) anchovies (about 12 fillets)
2 garlic cloves
¼ cup (60 mL) extra-virgin olive oil
2 tablespoons (30 mL) mayonnaise
1 tablespoon (15 mL) Dijon mustard
1 teaspoon (5 mL) pure liquid honey
1 teaspoon (5 mL) Worcestershire sauce
Zest and juice of 1 lemon
Freshly ground black pepper

FIRE-TOASTED CROUTONS
1 baguette, cut diagonally into 1-inch (2.5 cm) thick slices
2 tablespoons (30 mL) water, for brushing
2 tablespoons (30 mL) olive oil, for brushing
2 large garlic cloves, halved lengthwise
Sea salt
Freshly ground black pepper

GRILLED CAESAR SALAD
2 heads of romaine lettuce, quartered lengthwise
A 4-ounce (115 g) wedge of Parmigiano-Reggiano cheese
Freshly ground black pepper

GRILLING GREENS
Fire Cooking Method

Various savoury greens are easily grilled and wilted over a wood fire, their lightly bitter flavours enhanced by the flames. Romaine lettuce is often charred to add savoury flavours to a classic Caesar salad.

GRILLED KALE WITH CHARRED LEMON SESAME DRESSING

Kale's strong leaves and savoury flavour make it perfect for grilling. Over the fire the tough leaves wilt, their sweet flavours emerge, and their edges nicely crisp and char. A smoky dressing brightened with grilled lemon balances the dish.

BUILD A FIRE
Build and tend an active fire in your firepit, bringing to medium-high heat with live flame and a growing bed of glowing hot coals. Position a lightly oiled grill grate directly over the fire. Alternatively, light your charcoal grill or fire up your gas grill to its highest setting.

GRILL THE LEMON AND MAKE THE GRILLED LEMON SESAME DRESSING
Place the lemon halves cut side down to one side of the grill and sear until caramelized and lightly charred, 5 minutes or so. With a pair of tongs, squeeze the lemon juice into a small bowl. Add the tahini, mayonnaise, olive oil, honey, sesame oil, soy sauce, and hot sauce. Whisk until smooth.

GRILL THE KALE
In a large bowl, toss the kale leaves with the vegetable oil, salt, and pepper until evenly coated. Place the leaves, a few at a time, in a single layer on the grill (reserve the bowl). Cook, turning once, until wilted and lightly crisped, just a few seconds each side.

Transfer the grilled leaves to the bowl, toss with the grilled lemon sesame dressing, and top with the black and white sesame seeds.

SERVES 4 TO 6

CHARRED LEMON SESAME DRESSING
1 lemon, halved
1 tablespoon (15 mL) tahini
1 tablespoon (15 mL) mayonnaise
1 tablespoon (15 mL) olive oil
1 tablespoon (15 mL) pure liquid honey
1 teaspoon (5 mL) sesame oil
1 teaspoon (5 mL) soy sauce
½ teaspoon (2 mL) of your favourite hot sauce

GRILLED KALE
1 large bunch of kale (about 1 pound/ 450 g), leaves separated, centre ribs removed
2 tablespoons (30 mL) vegetable oil
Sea salt
Freshly ground black pepper
1 tablespoon (15 mL) black sesame seeds
1 tablespoon (15 mL) white sesame seeds

GRILLING LEMON
Fire Cooking Method

Grilling a lemon softens its flesh enough to fully release all its juices. Grilling adds caramelized flavour and releases fragrant lemon oil. This simple method is easy with any grilling fire as a last-second, flavourful dressing for vegetables.

WOOD-GRILLED ASPARAGUS AND BARLEY WALNUT SALAD WITH MISO DRESSING

Grilled asparagus seared yet simultaneously crisp, green, and tender, tossed together with chewy barley, sweet walnuts, and a bracing savoury dressing.

PREP THE BARLEY
In a medium saucepan over medium-high heat, toast the barley, stirring until fragrant, 2 or 3 minutes. Add the water, salt, and bay leaf and bring to a full simmer. Reduce the heat, cover tightly, and simmer until the barley is tender yet chewy, 45 minutes or so. Remove the bay leaf. Drain well and reserve.

MAKE THE MISO DRESSING
In a small bowl, combine the olive oil, lemon zest and juice, garlic, miso, mustard, sesame oil, and soy sauce. Whisk together until smooth. Reserve.

BUILD A FIRE
Build and tend an active fire in your firepit, bringing to high heat with live flame and a growing bed of glowing hot coals. Position a lightly oiled grill grate directly over the fire. Alternatively, light your charcoal grill or fire up your gas grill to its highest setting.

GRILL THE VEGETABLES AND FINISH THE SALAD
On a baking sheet, sprinkle the asparagus with the olive oil, season with salt and pepper, and roll until evenly coated. Spread the asparagus in a single layer perpendicular to the grill grate. Sear over high heat, undisturbed, for a minute or two, then gently roll to the other side. Cook until bright green and just barely tender, just another minute or so. Transfer to a resting platter.

Stack the asparagus spears and slice crosswise into 4 pieces. Transfer to a salad bowl and lightly toss with the barley, walnuts, and miso dressing.

SERVES 4 TO 6

BARLEY WALNUT SALAD
1 cup (250 mL) barley
3 cups (750 mL) water
½ teaspoon (2 mL) sea salt
1 bay leaf
1 cup (250 mL) walnut halves, roughly chopped

MISO DRESSING
¼ cup (60 mL) extra-virgin olive oil
Zest and juice of 1 lemon
2 garlic cloves, finely grated with a microplane or finely minced
1 tablespoon (15 mL) white miso
1 teaspoon (5 mL) Dijon mustard
1 teaspoon (5 mL) toasted sesame oil
1 teaspoon (5 mL) soy sauce

WOOD-GRILLED ASPARAGUS
1 bunch of asparagus, woody ends trimmed
1 tablespoon (15 mL) olive oil
Sea salt
Freshly ground black pepper

GRILLING ASPARAGUS
Vegetable Cooking Method

Asparagus cooked until bright green and tender over the fierce searing heat of a grill. The light, distinctive flavour of this vegetable is easily lost in boiling water and thus benefits from dry searing heat.

BROWN BUTTER SAGE CHANTERELLES

There's always room for another pan over the fire—especially a pan full of aromatic foraged mushrooms browned with butter and classic sage. This basic side dish deliciously partners any simple grilled meat and is easily adapted to any foraged or cultivated mushroom.

BUILD A FIRE

Build and tend an active fire in your firepit, bringing to medium-high heat with live flame and a growing bed of glowing hot coals. Position a grill grate directly over the fire. Alternatively, light your charcoal grill or fire up your gas grill to its highest setting.

BROWN THE BUTTER AND COOK THE MUSHROOMS

Toss the butter into a large cast-iron skillet over medium-high heat. Swirl gently as it melts, steams, foams, and eventually forms a flavourful brown sediment. Immediately toss in the sage leaves, swirling briefly, frying lightly, and perfuming the butter. Add the chanterelles, season with salt and pepper, and sauté until tender and juicy, just 3 or 4 minutes. At first, the mushrooms will absorb the fat and seem to dry out, but as they heat through, they'll very quickly start to release their moisture, becoming juicy and delicious. When they do, stir in the sherry vinegar. Keep an eye on the pan—cooked too far, the mushrooms rapidly release all their water and dry out yet again.

SERVES 4 TO 6

4 tablespoons (60 mL) salted butter

12 fresh sage leaves, stacked and thinly sliced

1 pound (450 g) fresh chanterelle mushrooms, cleaned and trimmed

½ teaspoon (2 mL) sea salt

Freshly ground black pepper

1 teaspoon (5 mL) sherry vinegar

BROWNING BUTTER
Fire Cooking Method

To unlock the full flavour potential of butter beyond its obvious but bland richness. To first evaporate the water within butter, allowing the remaining fat to carefully rise in temperature, flavourfully browning the milk solids. A quick cooking technique that must be halted at the point of perfection before browning becomes blackening.

GARLIC THYME CAMPFIRE POTATOES

Steak on the menu? This classic party trick adds familiar potatoes to the feast while keeping the cooking (and the party) focused on the fire.

2 pounds (900 g) medium Yukon Gold or large red potatoes (about 8 medium potatoes), quartered, or whole baby or fingerling potatoes
8 garlic cloves, halved
2 tablespoons (30 mL) olive oil
2 tablespoons (30 mL) fresh thyme leaves
1 teaspoon (5 mL) sea salt
Freshly ground black pepper

PREP THE POTATOES
Cut four 16-inch (40 cm) squares of heavy-duty foil. Lightly mist each sheet of foil with cooking spray.

In a large bowl, toss together the potatoes, garlic, olive oil, thyme, salt, and pepper. Tightly arrange the potatoes, skin side down if cut, in the middle of each sheet of foil. Join the top and bottom edges of the foil to form a package, tightly sealing the lengthwise centre seam, then fold the sides over the top.

BUILD A FIRE
Build and tend an active fire in your firepit, bringing to medium-high heat with live flame and a growing bed of glowing hot coals. Position a grill grate directly over the fire. Alternatively, light your charcoal grill or fire up your gas grill to its highest setting.

COOK THE POTATOES
Position the foil packages seam side up on the grill near but not directly over the live flames. Cook, rotating and repositioning frequently but not flipping, embracing the heat but avoiding the flames, until the potatoes are tender, 30 minutes or so. Let the packages rest in a warm place near the fire at least 15 minutes more.

FOIL PACKAGES
Fire Cooking Method

A tight enclosure that retains moisture and protects ingredients from the direct heat of the fire during sustained cooking. Heavy-duty aluminum foil is easily folded into a mini oven, then unfolded into a fireside plate after cooking.

GRILLED ZUCCHINI STEAKS WITH THYME BASTING SAUCE

Garden-fresh zucchini grilled over live flame while being basted with fragrant thyme sauce. The vegetable's dense texture is transformed by the heat while absorbing the buttery sauce.

BUILD A FIRE

Build and tend an active fire in your firepit, bringing to medium heat with some flame and a growing bed of glowing hot coals. Position a lightly oiled grill grate directly over the fire. Alternatively, light your charcoal grill or fire up your gas grill to its highest setting.

MAKE THE THYME BASTING SAUCE

In a small saucepan over medium heat, combine the butter, olive oil, mustard, shallot, garlic, and lemon zest and juice. Whisk together until the butter melts and a smooth sauce forms. Stir in the thyme and bay leaf and let rest in a warm place near the fire until needed.

GRILL THE ZUCCHINI

Lightly season the zucchini halves with salt and pepper. Place over medium heat, cut side up and close to each other in a single layer perpendicular to the grill grates. Using a heatproof silicone brush or small spoon, drizzle with the thyme basting sauce, coating the surface evenly, allowing the sauce to penetrate. Turn occasionally and continue basting until charred, tender, and lightly browned, 10 minutes or so. Serve immediately drizzled with any remaining basting sauce.

SERVES 4 TO 6

THYME BASTING SAUCE
½ cup (125 mL) butter
¼ cup (60 mL) olive oil
2 tablespoons (30 mL) Dijon mustard
1 shallot, minced
1 garlic clove, finely grated with
    a microplane or finely minced
Zest and juice of 1 lemon
1 tablespoon (15 mL) minced fresh thyme,
    a few sprigs reserved for garnish
1 bay leaf

ZUCCHINI STEAKS
4 zucchini, trimmed and halved
    lengthwise
Sea salt
Freshly ground black pepper

BASTING SAUCE
Fire Kitchen Ingredient

A moist, fragrant sauce applied directly and continuously to food as it cooks, best applied to absorbent ingredients during slow cooking methods.

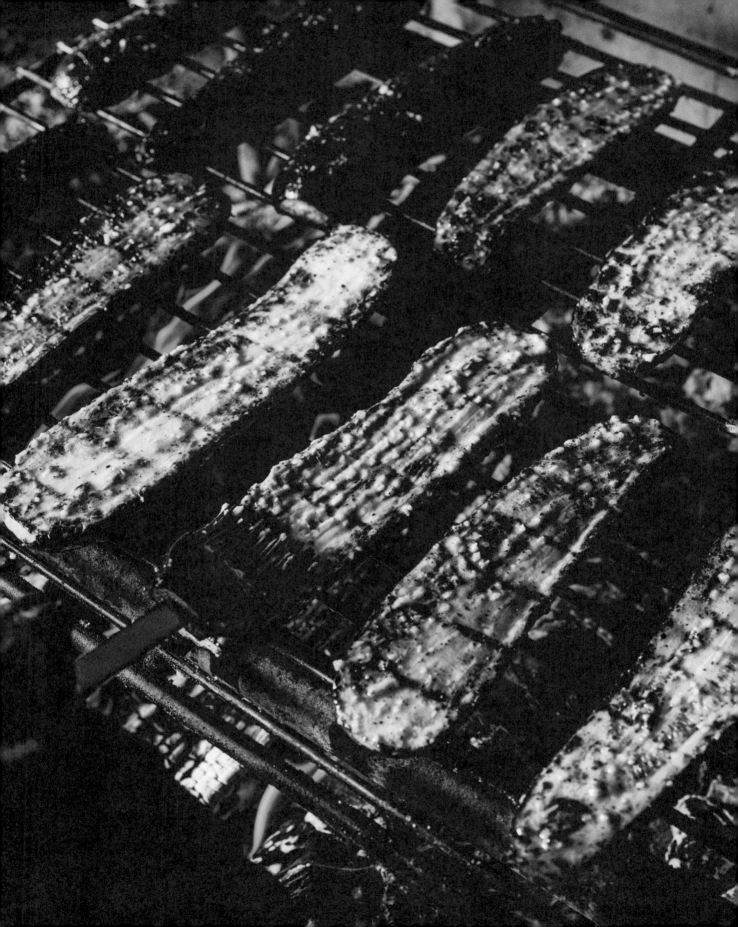

WOOD-FIRED SIPS AND SWEETS

SMOKY MANHATTAN

The aromatic complexity of wood and smoke have a natural affinity for the world of spirits and cocktails. There are many authentic ways to creatively flavour a cocktail with smoke beyond just waving around showy smouldering sprigs of dry herbs. Because bourbon is aged in charred oak barrels, it pairs naturally with smoky flavours.

SERVES 1

SPECIAL EQUIPMENT NEEDED: offset smokehouse; standard untreated cedar shingle

2 ounces of your favourite bourbon
1 ounce sweet vermouth
2 dashes of Angostura bitters
Smouldering hay sprig, for garnish

BUILD A FIRST FIRE
Build and tend a slow, smouldering fire in the firebox of your offset smokehouse. Use your favourite smoking wood (see page 4) to create a slow, steady stream of aromatic smoke.

MAKE THE SMOKED ICE
Pour 1 inch (2.5 cm) of water into a large roasting or baking pan and carefully position within the smoky chamber. Smoke the water, disturbing the surface once or twice, infusing the liquid with aromatic flavour, 15 minutes. Strain through a fine-mesh strainer into a large bowl. Carefully transfer the smoked water into ball or cube-shaped ice moulds and freeze solid.

BUILD A SECOND FIRE
Build and tend an active fire in your firepit, bringing to medium heat with a glowing bed of hot coals. Use a pair of metal tongs to handle the glowing live embers.

SMOKE THE GLASS
Position a small live ember on a standard untreated cedar shingle. Sprinkle with cedar shavings and lightly fan until smouldering. Cover the works with a cocktail glass and let fill with smoke. Working quickly, lift the glass straight up and slip a coaster under the open end to contain the smoke. Set on the bar surface. Refresh the glowing ember and cedar smoke as needed.

CRAFT THE COCKTAIL
Measure the bourbon, vermouth, and bitters into a mixing glass with ice. Stir briefly to chill. Gently lift and invert the smoke-filled jar and strain the cocktail into it. Cover tightly and swirl for 30 seconds. Pour into the cocktail glass and garnish with a smouldering hay sprig.

COCKTAIL SMOKE
Fire Kitchen Flavour

Smoke used as a flavourful cocktail ingredient. The nuanced aromas of various specific wood smokes can easily be shared in a variety of creative forms: infused liquids, syrups, spirits, and ice, even a thin film on the inside surface of a glass. Smoke is better absorbed by water than by alcohol and lingers within glassware.

IRON-SEARED BOURBON-SPICED MULLED CIDER

Classic cider and warm wine gently mulled with savoury herbs, aromatic spices, and sweet brown sugar. Spectacularly finished with a splash of bourbon and the searing heat of a cherry-red metal poker.

BUILD A FIRE

Build and tend an active fire in your firepit, bringing to medium-high heat with live flame and a growing bed of glowing hot coals. Position a grill grate directly over the fire. Position an iron or steel rod within the hot coals and preheat until glowing red.

MULL THE CIDER

In a Dutch oven, combine the cider, wine, brown sugar, bay leaves, rosemary, cinnamon, allspice, cloves, and chili flakes. Position over the fire's heat and bring the mixture to a full simmer. Cover tightly, remove from the heat, and let rest for 30 minutes or so, until the party requires mulled cider. The cider can be mulled up to 5 days in advance and refrigerated. Reheat when needed.

SEAR THE CIDER

Fill your favourite large mug with mulled cider. Top with your favourite bourbon, leaving room for the poker. Carefully plunge the hot rod into the cider, vigorously searing and caramelizing it, 15 seconds or so. Reheat the rod and repeat.

SERVES 4 TO 8

SPECIAL EQUIPMENT NEEDED: cast-iron Dutch oven, round iron rod or heavy steel poker, 1 inch (2.5 cm) thick × 18 inches (46 cm) long

4 cups (1 L) fresh apple cider
2 cups (500 mL) red or white wine
½ cup (125 mL) firmly packed brown sugar
2 bay leaves
2 sprigs of fresh rosemary
1 teaspoon (5 mL) cinnamon
½ teaspoon (2 mL) ground allspice
¼ teaspoon (1 mL) ground cloves
¼ teaspoon (1 mL) red chili flakes
4 ounces of your favourite bourbon or whisky

IRON-SEARING LIQUID
Fire Cooking Method

To insert a very hot iron poker directly into mulled cider or other flavourful liquid. The metal is heated in a fire until glowing cherry red, then plunged into the cider. The intensely hot metal heats the cider, caramelizing its sugars and deepening its flavours.

IRON-CRUSTED CARAMEL CRÈME BRÛLÉE

My classic crème brûlée includes an extra caramel twist: the custard is flavoured with caramelized sugar before the sugary topping is traditionally browned. A modern kitchen blowtorch works well, but over the centuries pastry chefs relied on a simple tool to reliably brown the crispy, crackly surface: infrared heat from a disc of glowing hot metal.

Preheat the oven to 325°F (160°C). Bring a kettleful of water to a boil.

MAKE THE CARAMEL BASE
Pour ½ cup (125 mL) water into a small saucepan over medium-high heat. Pour the sugar into the centre of the water and without disturbing, bring to a vigorous simmer. Continue cooking as the water bubbles away, the sugar melts, and the syrup begins to lightly colour. Begin to swirl gently until deep golden brown and aromatic, then carefully pour in the cream. Reduce the heat to low and whisk until smooth and simmering again. Whisk in the milk and remove from the heat.

MAKE THE CUSTARD BASE
In a medium bowl, whisk together the egg yolks, vanilla, and salt. Slowly whisk in a ladleful of the hot caramel mixture. Continue whisking in a ladleful at a time, gradually raising the temperature of the mixture without scrambling the eggs.

BAKE THE CUSTARD
Divide the custard mixture among a set of shallow ramekins or pour into a single shallow baking dish. Carefully transfer to a pan just large enough to hold the ramekins or dish. Pour enough boiling water into the pan to come two-thirds up the sides of the ramekins or dish. Bake until the custard is firm but still a touch jiggly in the centre, 30 to 40 minutes. Remove from the water and refrigerate, uncovered, until chilled and firm, a few hours, even overnight.

BUILD A FIRE
Build and tend an active fire in your firepit, bringing to high heat with live flame and a growing bed of glowing hot coals. Position a brûlée iron within the hot coals and preheat until glowing red.

BRÛLÉE THE TOP
Sprinkle the turbinado sugar over the surface of a chilled custard, gently tilting back and forth until completely covered. Tip the excess sugar out onto the next ramekin and continue until all are evenly covered. Working with 1 custard at a time, remove the brûlée iron from the fire and hold it ½ inch (1 cm) above the surface. Watch carefully as the sugar melts, bubbles, and browns. Remove the iron when the crust is perfectly golden brown. Repeat with remaining custards, reheating the iron each time. Serve immediately or refrigerate for a few hours before serving.

MAKES 4 TO 6 INDIVIDUAL CRÈME BRÛLÉES OR 1 LARGE BRÛLÉE

SPECIAL EQUIPMENT NEEDED: brûlée iron with handle, 6 inches (15 cm) wide and ½ inch (1 cm) thick

CUSTARD BASE
½ cup (125 mL) water
½ cup (125 mL) white sugar
1 cup (250 mL) heavy (35%) cream
1 cup (250 mL) 2% milk
6 large egg yolks
1 teaspoon (5 mL) pure vanilla extract
¼ teaspoon (1 mL) salt

BRÛLÉED TOP
½ cup (125 mL) turbinado or other coarse granulated sugar

BRÛLÉE IRON
Fire Kitchen Tool

A simple disc of thick, heavy steel or iron heated until glowing hot, then held just above an ingredient or prepared food until the surface below toasts, caramelizes, or browns. The metal does not come in direct contact with the food.

CAMPFIRE BAKED APPLES WITH
WHISKY WALNUT BUTTER

Apples scented with cinnamon and whisky, stuffed with a sweet, buttery walnut filling, and baked by the fire with the slower pace of indirect heat.

PREP THE APPLES

Using a small paring knife, neatly cut the core out from each apple without cutting through its bottom, forming a deep hollow within the centre. Using the point of a thermometer, lightly poke each apple a dozen times within the hole. Pour ½ ounce of the whisky into each apple, turning the fruit so the liquid finds its way into the holes.

In a small bowl, stir together the butter, walnuts, brown sugar, and cinnamon. Fill the apples evenly with the mixture.

BUILD A FIRE

Build and tend an active fire in your firepit, bringing to medium heat with a glowing bed of hot coals. Position a grill grate next to the fire for indirect heat.

BAKE THE APPLES

Carefully place the apples on the grate in the indirect heat of the fire. Close the lid if you have one. Slowly bake until the sugary filling caramelizes and the apples are bubbling and tender, 20 minutes or so. Serve each apple sliced in half.

SERVES 4 TO 8

4 large baking apples (Honeycrisp, Cortland, Braeburn, or Granny Smith)

2 ounces of your favourite whisky, divided

4 tablespoons (60 mL) butter, softened

½ cup (125 mL) chopped walnuts

½ cup (125 mL) lightly packed brown sugar

1 teaspoon (5 mL) cinnamon

FIRE BAKING
Fire Cooking Method

Harnessing the indirect low heat of a fire to slowly cook ingredients that would be damaged by direct high roasting heat. Cooking within the lower heat baking zone to the side of an active cooking fire.

FLAMING STRAWBERRY SHORTCAKES
WITH TARRAGON WHIPPED CREAM

The classic strawberry shortcake elevated with a variety of licorice-like flavours, flourishes, and flambéed fruit. Warm fruit flambéed in an improvised syrup, easy spiced cream biscuits with a sugary crust, and pillowy soft whipped cream intriguingly scented with tarragon.

MAKE THE BISCUITS

Preheat the oven to 425°F (220°C). Turn on the convection fan if you have one. Line a baking sheet with a silicone baking mat or parchment paper.

In a large bowl, whisk together the flour, white sugar, baking powder, star anise, and salt. Pour in the cream and vanilla. Using the handle of a wooden spoon, vigorously stir until a coarse dough forms. Lightly flour your hands and a work surface. Turn the dough out onto the work surface and knead a few times into a smooth, firm dough.

Pat or roll the dough into an even 1½-inch (4 cm) thick disc. Cut into 12 even wedges and transfer to the lined baking sheet. Spread the raw sugar, fennel seeds, and anise seeds on a small plate. Lightly brush the top of each biscuit with some melted butter, then carefully dip the sticky surface into the sugar mixture, gently shaking off any excess. Return to the baking sheet, evenly spaced. Bake until golden brown and crispy, 20 minutes or so. Transfer to a rack. Serve warm or let cool and store in a tightly sealed resealable plastic bag at room temperature for up to 3 days.

MAKE THE TARRAGON WHIPPED CREAM

In a chilled large bowl, whip the cream, sugar, vanilla, and tarragon until soft and thick. Refrigerate until needed.

BUILD A FIRE

Build and tend an active fire in your firepit, bringing to medium heat with a glowing bed of hot coals. Position a large cast-iron plancha or skillet over the fire and preheat.

SERVES 12

SPECIAL EQUIPMENT NEEDED: large cast-iron plancha or skillet

SPICED BISCUITS

4 cups (1 L) all-purpose flour
¼ cup (60 mL) white sugar
2 tablespoons (30 mL) baking powder
1 tablespoon (15 mL) ground star anise
¼ teaspoon (1 mL) salt
2½ cups (625 mL) heavy (35%) cream
1 teaspoon (5 mL) pure vanilla extract
2 tablespoons (30 mL) raw sugar
1 tablespoon (15 mL) fennel seeds
1 tablespoon (15 mL) anise seeds
1 tablespoon (15 mL) butter, melted

TARRAGON WHIPPED CREAM

3 cups (750 mL) heavy (35%) cream
3 tablespoons (45 mL) white sugar
1 teaspoon (5 mL) pure vanilla extract
Leaves and tender stems from 1 bunch of fresh tarragon, finely chopped, a few sprigs reserved for garnish

FLAMING STRAWBERRIES

4 pounds (1.8 kg) fresh strawberries, hulled and halved
1 cup (250 mL) white sugar
8 tablespoons (125 mL) butter, softened
1 cup (250 mL) Pernod, Sambuca, ouzo, or other anise liqueur
Zest and juice of 1 lemon

Recipe continues

249

FLAMBÉ THE STRAWBERRIES

In a medium bowl, toss the strawberries with the sugar until evenly combined. Toss the butter onto the hot plancha. Swirl gently as it melts, steams, foams, and eventually lightly browns. Add the strawberries, swirling and tossing until sizzling.

Extend your arm, swing the sizzling pan away from the flame, and tilt the far edge down and away from you. Pour the liqueur into the far corner with the strawberries. Keeping your arm extended, tilt the pan towards the flame until the rapidly evaporating alcohol ignites. Hold steadily as the flames and applause erupt. Sauté as the flames die down and the flavours build, a minute or so longer. Stir in the lemon zest and juice.

ASSEMBLE THE SHORTCAKES

Cut the shortcakes in half with a serrated knife. Position the bottom half of the biscuits on individual plates. Divide the warm strawberries between the biscuits. Top with a dollop of tarragon whipped cream. Position the top half of the biscuit on top and garnish with a tarragon sprig.

FLAMBÉ
Fire Kitchen Method

The classic fiery finishing technique for igniting fruits, lighting up crêpes, and generally inciting mayhem. Warming highly flammable high-proof liqueur until its vapours evaporate and spectacularly ignite.

RUM CREAMSICLE CAMPFIRE MARSHMALLOWS

The very best days always end around a campfire full of family and friends toasting marshmallows. These homemade treats are so easy to make and even more fun to enjoy with your fire mates.

MAKE THE DUSTING POWDER

Sift together the icing sugar and cornstarch into a small bowl. Lightly oil a 9-inch (2.5 L) square baking pan. Dust with some of the powdery mixture, reserving the rest for the marshmallows.

MAKE THE MARSHMALLOWS

In a small saucepan, bring an inch (2.5 cm) or so of water to a simmer. Pour ¾ cup (175 mL) of the water into the bowl of a stand mixer. Sprinkle the gelatin over the water and stir it as best you can. (It will look lumpy and grainy.) Let the mixture rest as it hydrates, 5 minutes or so. Place the mixer bowl directly over the simmering water and gently stir until the gelatin is dissolved. Return the bowl to the mixer and fit it with the whisk.

Meanwhile, in another small saucepan, combine the remaining ½ cup + 2 tablespoons (155 mL) water with the corn syrup and sugar. Cook over medium heat, stirring occasionally as the sugar dissolves into a syrup. Continue as it simmers and rises in temperature. Wash down the sides occasionally with a moist pastry brush to keep crystals from forming. As soon as a candy thermometer registers exactly 245°F (118°C), remove from the heat.

With the mixer on medium speed, carefully pour the hot syrup into the gelatin mixture in a thin, continuous stream between the whisk and the side of the bowl. Increase the speed to high and continue beating until the mixture is thick and fluffy and cooled to room temperature, 10 minutes or so. Whisk in the rum, vanilla, and orange extracts. Scrape the mixture into the prepared baking pan. Spread evenly with a lightly oiled spatula. Let cool for an hour or so, then cover loosely with foil. Let sit at room temperature overnight to dry completely.

Lightly dust the marshmallows and your cutting board with some of the reserved dusting powder. Invert the pan and cut into squares with a sharp knife or kitchen scissors dusted with a bit more powder as you go: 3 cuts in each direction yields sixteen 2-inch (5 cm) square marshmallows, 4 cuts yields 25 medium, while 5 cuts in each direction will make 36 smaller ones. Generously dust the marshmallows all over with the remaining dusting powder. Store the marshmallows between layers of parchment paper in an airtight container at room temperature for up to 3 days.

MAKES 16 LARGE, 25 MEDIUM, OR 36 SMALL MARSHMALLOWS

SPECIAL EQUIPMENT NEEDED: candy thermometer

DUSTING POWDER

¼ cup (60 mL) icing sugar
¼ cup (60 mL) cornstarch

MARSHMALLOWS

¾ cup (175 mL) + ½ cup + 2 tablespoons (155 mL) water, divided
4 envelopes (1 ounce/7 g each) unflavoured gelatin
1⅓ cups (325 mL) light corn syrup
2 cups (500 mL) white sugar
2 tablespoons (30 mL) rum extract
1 tablespoon (15 mL) pure vanilla extract
1 teaspoon (5 mL) pure orange extract

Recipe continues

BUILD A FIRE

Build and tend an active campfire in your firepit, with live flame and a growing bed of glowing hot coals.

TOAST THE MARSHMALLOWS

Gather your friends and family, whittle a few sticks, and toast away, dipping in and out of the flames until evenly toasted to your liking.

MARSHMALLOW TOASTING
Fire Cooking Method

A simple yet infinitely variable method for caramelizing and warming a fluffy, sugary marshmallow. Experienced toasters tend to develop personal techniques for achieving the optimal balance of flame, char, and golden brown. Others perfect their bragging skills. All enjoy the spectacle.

CONDIMENT PANTRY

OLD-SCHOOL DRY RUB

This basic dry rub is an excellent all-purpose seasoning blend with a balanced aromatic flavour. Its sweet-salty-spicy taste is perfect for smoking projects.

In a small bowl, whisk together the brown sugar, salt, paprika, cayenne pepper, and ground bay leaf. Transfer to a mason jar, tightly seal, and store in a cool, dark place for up to 6 months.

MAKES 2 CUPS (500 ML)

1 cup (250 mL) packed brown sugar

¾ cup (175 mL) Diamond Crystal kosher salt

½ cup (125 mL) smoked paprika

¼ cup (60 mL) cayenne pepper

2 tablespoons (30 mL) ground bay leaf

BAY SPICE

Every fire chef has a personalized spice blend, a unique-to-them expression of aromatic flavour. This multi-purpose seasoning is an excellent finishing salt, poultry rub, or salmon cure. Make it yours and feel free to tweak the flavours.

In a spice grinder or dedicated coffee grinder, combine the peppercorns, bay leaves, fennel seeds, and coriander seeds and grind into a fine powder. Transfer to a food processor with the brown sugar and salt. Grind until evenly blended and fragrant. Transfer to a clean mason jar, tightly seal, and store in a cool, dark place for up to 3 months.

MAKES ABOUT 3 CUPS (750 ML)

¼ cup (60 mL) black peppercorns

12 bay leaves

3 tablespoons (45 mL) fennel seeds

3 tablespoons (45 mL) coriander seeds

2 cups (500 mL) firmly packed brown sugar

1 cup (250 mL) Diamond Crystal kosher salt

PRESERVED LEMON PURÉE

Our neighbour Louise is legendary for sharing her preserved lemons. They're insanely delicious, so rather than make our own we rely on her to keep us well stocked. For anyone who doesn't live next door, here's her recipe.

6 organic lemons, scrubbed and dried
3 tablespoons (45 mL) coarse sea salt
1 tablespoon (15 mL) coriander seeds
1 bay leaf

Quarter 3 of the lemons lengthwise, stopping about ½ inch (1 cm) from the bottom so they stay intact. Working with 1 lemon at a time over a small bowl to catch any juices, gently spread open the lemon and remove as many seeds as you can. Sprinkle in 1 tablespoon (15 mL) or so of the salt and some coriander seeds. Close the lemon back up, massaging the salt into the flesh and skin. Repeat with the other 2 quartered lemons. Pack and squish the lemons into a 2-cup (500 mL) mason jar along with the bay leaf and any remaining coriander seeds.

Zest and juice the remaining 3 lemons into the same bowl. Pour into the jar along with any accumulated salt. If the lemons are not submerged in juice, add more until they're covered. Screw the lid on tightly and give the jar a good shake. Refrigerate the lemons for 4 to 6 weeks, shaking and inverting the jar every few days.

After preserving, transfer the lemons and juice to a blender or food processor, discarding the bay leaf and any lemon seeds you come across. Purée until smooth. Store in a clean mason jar in the refrigerator for up to 1 year.

PICKLED RED ONIONS

This ubiquitous condiment has been a part of the inn's pantry for thirty years. Its bright flavour and crisp texture balances many of our improvised vegetable salads and sides.

1 cup (250 mL) red wine vinegar
1 cup (250 mL) sugar
1 tablespoon (15 mL) fennel seeds
1 tablespoon (15 mL) coriander seeds
2 bay leaves
2 or 3 red onions, thinly sliced

Measure the red wine vinegar, sugar, fennel seeds, coriander seeds, and bay leaves into a medium saucepan. Bring to a full boil over medium-high heat. Gently stir in the red onions. Cover tightly and remove from the heat. Let rest at room temperature until cool. Transfer to a 2-cup (500 mL) mason jar, tightly seal, and refrigerate overnight. The pickled onions are at their best after a few days resting and will last for up to 1 month.

SRIRACHA PICKLED RED ONIONS

This version of our classic condiment is updated with one of my favourite hot sauces. Sweet and sour and now spicy!

Measure the red wine vinegar, sugar, sriracha, and salt into a medium saucepan. Bring to a full boil over medium-high heat. Gently stir in the red onions. Cover tightly and remove from the heat. Let rest at room temperature until cool. Transfer to a 2-cup (500 mL) mason jar, tightly seal, and refrigerate overnight. The pickled onions are at their best after a few days resting and will last for up to 1 month.

MAKES 2 CUPS (500 ML)

1 cup (250 mL) red wine vinegar
1 cup (250 mL) sugar
1 tablespoon (15 mL) sriracha
¼ teaspoon (1 mL) sea salt
2 or 3 red onions, thinly sliced

MARITIME MUSTARD PICKLES

Chef Craig Flinn began his illustrious culinary career at the Inn at Bay Fortune long before becoming a cookbook author and legendary Nova Scotia chef. His gluten-free mustard pickles are the gold standard for the chutney-style version of this condiment we prefer. All the traditional flavours are included—there's just a bit more cheferly knife work. You'll be rewarded with a bright, distinctive all-purpose condiment and an authentic taste of the Maritimes.

BRINE THE VEGETABLES
In a medium pot, bring the water and salt to a full boil. In a medium bowl, stir together the cucumbers, onions, celery, and bell peppers. Pour the boiling salted water over the vegetables. Let rest for 2 hours. Drain well.

PICKLE AND PRESERVE THE VEGETABLES
In a large pot, stir together the sugar, white vinegar, mustard seeds, dry mustard, turmeric, cumin, fenugreek, and chili flakes. Reserve 2 cups (500 mL) of the mixture. Add the drained vegetables to the pot and bring to a full boil over high heat. Reduce to a simmer and cook until tender, flavourful, and reduced, 15 minutes. Meanwhile, stir and dissolve the cornstarch into the reserved vinegar mixture, forming a slurry. Return the heat to high, stir in the cornstarch slurry, and cook, stirring constantly, until noticeably thickened, 2 or 3 minutes. Remove from the heat. Divide among mason jars or resealable containers and refrigerate until cool and thickened further, at least 2 hours, even overnight. Pickles will keep for several weeks.

MAKES 12 CUPS (3 L)

3 cups (750 mL) water
½ cup (125 mL) Diamond Crystal kosher salt
3 English cucumbers, unpeeled, seeded and finely diced
4 yellow onions, finely diced
2 celery stalks, finely diced
1 green bell pepper, stem, seeds, and pith discarded, finely diced
1 red bell pepper, stem, seeds, and pith discarded, finely diced
4 cups (1 L) sugar
3 cups (750 mL) white vinegar
2 tablespoons (30 mL) yellow mustard seeds
2 tablespoons (30 mL) dry mustard
2 tablespoons (30 mL) ground turmeric
1 tablespoon (15 mL) ground cumin
1 tablespoon (15 mL) ground fenugreek
1 tablespoon (15 mL) red chili flakes
½ cup (125 mL) cornstarch

CLASSIC CHIMICHURRI

Chimichurri is Argentina's gift to the fire cook's condiment pantry. This punchy sauce is herbaceously green and never cooked.

In a small food processor, combine the onion, garlic, red wine vinegar, and olive oil and process until smooth. Add the oregano, paprika, cumin, salt, chili flakes, parsley, and water. Process until the leaves are finely chopped. Transfer to a small serving bowl, cover, and let rest until the flavours have a chance to develop, at least a few hours, even overnight. Leftovers can be refrigerated for several weeks.

MAKES 2 CUPS (500 ML)

1 medium white or yellow onion, peeled and quartered

4 garlic cloves

¼ cup (60 mL) red wine vinegar

¼ cup (60 mL) extra-virgin olive oil

2 tablespoons (30 mL) dried oregano

1 tablespoon (15 mL) smoked paprika

1 teaspoon (5 mL) ground cumin

1 teaspoon (5 mL) sea salt

½ teaspoon (2 mL) red chili flakes

Leaves and tender stems from 1 bunch of fresh flat-leaf or curly parsley

¼ cup (60 mL) water

MINT CHIMICHURRI

This version of classic Argentinean chimichurri is made with aromatic mint to serve with any lamb dish.

In a small food processor, combine the onion, garlic, red wine vinegar, olive oil, cumin, salt, and chili flakes. Process until smooth. Add the mint and water. Process until the leaves are finely chopped. Transfer to a small serving bowl, cover, and let rest until the flavours have a chance to develop, at least a few hours, even overnight. Leftovers can be refrigerated for several weeks.

MAKES 2 CUPS (500 ML)

1 medium white or yellow onion, peeled and quartered

4 garlic cloves

¼ cup (60 mL) red wine vinegar

¼ cup (60 mL) extra-virgin olive oil

1 teaspoon (5 mL) ground cumin

1 teaspoon (5 mL) sea salt

½ teaspoon (2 mL) red chili flakes

Leaves and tender stems from 1 large bunch of fresh mint

¼ cup (60 mL) water

CLASSIC BUFFALO SAUCE

The sauce that launched a revolution—simply delicious, deliciously simple. For the most authentic flavour, stick to Frank's Original Red Hot Sauce, but any relatively mild hot sauce works well.

MAKES ALMOST A CUP (200 ML)

⅓ cup (75 mL) butter
½ cup (125 mL) Frank's RedHot Original Hot Sauce or other mild hot sauce

In a small saucepan, gently melt the butter over low heat. Remove from the heat and whisk in the hot sauce. To sauce wings, rewarm as needed just before tossing.

ANCHO BARBECUE SAUCE

Our classic all-purpose barbecue sauce, deeply flavoured with aromatic medium-heat ancho chilies, ready for dipping or brushing over the fire. Ancho chili peppers are dried medium-heat poblano peppers. They're not as spicy as chipotles dried from jalapeños.

MAKES 4 CUPS (1 L)

1 can (28 ounces/796 mL) San Marzano tomatoes
Cloves from 1 head of garlic, thinly sliced
½ cup (125 mL) apple cider vinegar
½ cup (125 mL) firmly packed brown sugar
¼ cup (60 mL) yellow mustard
1 tablespoon (15 mL) Worcestershire sauce
1 tablespoon (15 mL) ground cumin
1 teaspoon (5 mL) cinnamon
4 ounces (115 g) dry ancho chili peppers, stems and seeds discarded, broken into small flakes

Pour the tomatoes into a medium saucepan and crush them with your fingers or a potato masher. Add the garlic, cider vinegar, brown sugar, mustard, Worcestershire sauce, cumin, and cinnamon. Bring to a full simmer over medium-high heat, stirring frequently. Stir in the chilies, cover tightly, remove from the heat, and let rest for an hour or so while the chilies rehydrate and soften.

Purée until smooth with an immersion blender or in a high-speed blender. Use immediately or transfer to a mason jar or other airtight container, seal tightly, and refrigerate for up to 1 month.

CHIPOTLE BARBECUE SAUCE

A spicier version of our classic all-purpose barbecue sauce, brightly flavoured with smoky chipotle chilies, the dried version of a jalapeño pepper.

Pour the tomatoes into a medium saucepan and crush them with your fingers or a potato masher. Add the garlic, cider vinegar, brown sugar, mustard, Worcestershire sauce, cumin, and cinnamon. Bring to a full simmer over medium-high heat, stirring frequently. Stir in the chilies, cover tightly, remove from the heat, and let rest for an hour or so while the chilies rehydrate and soften.

Purée until smooth with an immersion blender or in a high-speed blender. Use immediately or transfer to a mason jar or other airtight container, seal tightly, and refrigerate for up to 1 month.

MAKES 4 CUPS (1 L)

1 can (28 ounces/796 mL) San Marzano tomatoes

Cloves from 1 head of garlic, thinly sliced

½ cup (125 mL) apple cider vinegar

½ cup (125 mL) firmly packed brown sugar

¼ cup (60 mL) yellow mustard

1 tablespoon (15 mL) Worcestershire sauce

1 tablespoon (15 mL) ground cumin

1 teaspoon (5 mL) cinnamon

4 ounces (115 g) dried chipotle chili peppers, stems and seeds removed, broken into small flakes

GOCHUJANG GINGER SAUCE

The warm heat and wonderful aromatic flavour of traditionally fermented Korean gochujang paste earns it a place of prominence in the fire pantry. Here it shines within a brightly balanced barbecue sauce on hand for dipping or glazing.

In a large bowl, combine the gochujang, ketchup, ginger, brown sugar, fish sauce, and rice wine vinegar. Whisk until a smooth sauce forms. Transfer to a mason jar or other airtight container, seal tightly, and refrigerate for up to 1 month.

To finish a grilled dish, toss at the last second with the sauce, return to the grill to glaze if you like, and sprinkle with sesame seeds and green onions before serving.

MAKES 1 CUP (250 ML)

¼ cup (60 mL) gochujang

¼ cup (60 mL) ketchup

2 tablespoons (30 mL) finely grated frozen ginger (about 1 ounce/28 g)

2 tablespoons (30 mL) brown sugar

2 tablespoons (30 mL) fish sauce

2 tablespoons (30 mL) rice wine vinegar

2 tablespoons (30 mL) white sesame seeds, for serving

2 green onions, very thinly sliced, for serving

SPECIAL INGREDIENTS, RESOURCES, AND CONTACTS

Many of the recipes and techniques in this book rely on specific gear or a particular ingredient from a special supplier. Here are some suggestions.

BIG GREEN EGG AND OTHER KAMADO GRILLS

Canadian Tire

Home Hardware

Home Depot

biggreenegg.ca

CAST-IRON COOKWARE

Lodge Cast Iron

South Pittsburg, Tennessee

lodgecastiron.com

FIRE-COOKING GEAR

Bass Pro Shops

basspro.com

Cabelas

cabelas.ca

DIGITAL THERMOMETERS

ThermoWorks

American Fork, Utah

thermoworks.com

FLAMBADOU

Pine Ridge Forge

Etsy.com

CHILI ROASTER

Santa Barbara Chili Roasters

Santa Barbara, California

santabarbarchiliroasters.com

VERTICAL SKEWER WITH ROASTING PAN

Amazon.ca

PINK CURING SALT

Amazon.ca

FRESH SALMON

Sustainable Blue

Centre Burlington, Nova Scotia

Sustainableblue.com

KONRO GRILLS, BINCHOTAN CHARCOAL, AND SPECIALTY PROFESSIONAL COOKWARE

The Cook's Edge

Charlottetown, Prince Edward Island

thecooksedge.com

SPECIAL THANKS

To all who contributed so mightily to this book and to all we do together at the Inn at Bay Fortune. Chef Chris's leadership and culinary insight, Farmer Kevin's bounty, Jason's creativity and hand modelling skills, Matt's mushrooms, Phil's dull chainsaw, Jerry's endless woodpile, and anyone who ever humped a load of wood at the inn.

Thank you, Adrianna, for so graciously embracing this project with your own eloquent artisanship and eye for detail. Thanks, Al—yet again—for your mighty vision and tireless artistry. Merci beaucoup, Jennifer, for managing the madness. I'm proud of you team!

Thank you, our guests, for filling our tables, savouring our flavours, and supporting our vision. We're eternally grateful for what we've learned through serving you.

Thank you most of all to my family, for years of fires and inspiring me every day, Gabe, Ariella, Camille, and to my amazing wife Chazz for keeping my hottest fire burning.

INDEX